AS GOOD
AS SHE
IMAGINED

AS GOOD AS SHE IMAGINED

THE REDEEMING STORY OF THE ANGEL OF TUCSON
CHRISTINA-TAYLOR GREEN

ROXANNA GREEN

WITH JERRY B. JENKINS

WORTHY
PUBLISHING

Published by Worthy Publishing, a division of Worthy Media, Inc., 134 Franklin Road, Suite 200, Brentwood, Tennessee 37027.

HELPING PEOPLE EXPERIENCE THE HEART OF GOD

eBook available at www.worthypublishing.com

Audio distributed through Oasis Audio; visit www.oasisaudio.com

Library of Congress Control Number: 2011941016

For foreign and subsidiary rights, contact Riggins International Rights Services, Inc.; www.rigginsrights.com

ISBN: 978-1-61795-012-4 (hardcover w/ jacket)
ISBN: 978-1-61795-086-5 (international trade paper)

Cover Design: Christopher Tobias
Front Cover Photo: Courtesy of the Green family
Back Cover Photo: © 2010 Jon Wolf
Interior Design and Typesetting: Susan Browne Design

Printed in the United States of America

11 12 13 14 15 16 17 RRD 8 7 6 5 4 3 2 1

To the memory of my mother
Yolanda M. Segalini (1935-2009)
And with thanks to my brothers
Paul and Gregory Segalini
for their love and support
R.G.

And with appreciation for
Kevin Leman
J.B.J.

CONTENTS

THE MACABRE SETTING

Stories of horror are rarely set in idyllic Tucson, Arizona. That town, affectionately known by the locals as T-Town or the Old Pueblo, became—in one horrific fusillade from an automatic weapon—a metaphor for the worldwide battle between good and evil, leaving residents and visitors shaking their heads even a year later.

Tucson comprises just under 200 square miles of beautiful, arid land about 2,400 feet above sea level and is home to more than a million people. Its name comes from the old Uto-Aztecan and means "spring at the base of the black hill," referring to a nearby volcanic mountain. Residents enjoy nearly 360-degree mountain views.

Lying just sixty miles north of Mexico, Tucson vibrates with a rich history of Hispanic and Latino influence, more than 35 percent of its population Mexican-American.

On Tucson's northwest side lies its oldest suburb, Casas Adobes, which arose in the late 1940s. The parking lot of a typical suburban grocery store there, the Safeway at La Toscana Village, appears the most unlikely setting for mass murder, a calamity that would rock a nation.

And for a nine-year-old girl, ironically born just hours before the atrocities of 9/11/01, to instantly come to represent all innocent children who suffer at the hands of corrupt, radical, or delusional adults . . . well, Tucson—and America—are still reeling.

Seek the Kingdom of God above all else, and live righteously, and he will give you everything you need. So don't worry about tomorrow, for tomorrow will bring its own worries. Today's trouble is enough for today.

Matthew 6:33-34 (nlt)

People forget that a state known for triple-digit dry heat can be mild and beautiful in the winter. At 7:25 a.m. on that fateful Saturday, January 8, 2011, Tucson, Arizona, dawns just above freezing.

CHAPTER ONE

"SOMEONE WILL SPEAK WITH YOU"

YEA, THOUGH I WALK THROUGH THE VALLEY OF THE SHADOW OF DEATH, I WILL FEAR NO EVIL; FOR YOU ARE WITH ME (PSALM 23:4A).

I'll never forget the phone call from Suzi Hileman's husband, Bill. It was 10:30 in the morning, Saturday, January 8, 2011.

"Roxanna, listen," he said, his voice tight. "I just got a call that Suzi and Christina are at the University Medical Center."

Suzi, a neighbor and friend, had taken my nine-year-old daughter, Christina-Taylor, to an outdoor event hosted by Congresswoman Gabrielle Giffords.

"What happened?" I said. "An accident?"

"I wasn't told anything, just that we need to get there."

The drive to the UMC would take me right past where Suzi and Christina-Taylor were to have seen the congresswoman.

I told my son, Dallas, "Get your shoes on and grab a jacket, because we have to go to the hospital."

"What's going on, Mom?"

"I'm not sure. Just pray everything will be okay, all right?"

We don't wear it on our sleeves, but praying is a normal thing for our family. Dallas and I were both praying silently, hardly knowing what to ask for.

I called my husband, John, but had to leave a message; we had to get going. As I neared the Safeway in La Toscana Village Mall, I saw emergency vehicles, flashing lights, and barricades. I was going to have to go the back way.

I wound up on the south end of the strip mall and saw people wandering about and yellow police tape around the plaza. If Suzi's little car had gotten caught in a major pileup, maybe it was a more serious accident than I thought.

Christina-Taylor and Suzi had to be okay though, right? That's not my life; serious things don't happen to my family and friends.

I reached the hospital just before 11 a.m., but when I followed the signs to the emergency room, I found the entrance blocked off with police cars and ringed with camera crews and news trucks.

Suddenly I had a one-track mind. I needed to find a place to park so I could get in there and make sure Christina-Taylor was all right. I told myself everything would be all right once I reached her. I just wanted answers, to know my daughter was okay. I could deal with anything else, no matter how serious.

In the ER I went to a woman behind the counter and introduced myself. She said, "Wait here just a minute."

I was a nurse, not to mention a mother who had been to the ER before. That was not typical. I could tell by the way she looked at me that she knew exactly who Christina-Taylor was and what had happened to my daughter.

I didn't want to hear, "Wait a minute"; I wanted to hear, "Just one second."

When the woman returned, I couldn't get a thing out of her. She looked as if she would rather be anywhere but right there right then, and she led Dallas and me to the elevator and to a waiting room on the sixth floor. She asked if Dallas or I wanted anything to drink. I knew she was trying to be helpful, but something to drink was the last thing on my mind.

"What I want," I said, "is for you to tell me what has happened and what is going on with Christina-Taylor."

"I'm sorry, I can't," she said. "But someone is going to come and talk to you."

I didn't like where this was headed, but I did not even allow myself to think the worst. I was hoping for the best and working to stay calm. I sat down, more convinced than ever that whatever this was, it was worse than I had originally thought. I envisioned debilitating injuries, maybe a long recovery time. We would handle it; that was the kind of family we were.

I asked the woman to direct me to a restroom, and as I entered I imagined Christina-Taylor was in emergency surgery. That had to be why I was not being told anything yet; no one knew anything.

I realized this was probably going to be the last time I would be alone before someone came to talk to us. I was desperate and glad Dallas didn't have to see me that way. I knelt on the floor and folded my hands. "Lord," I said, "please take care of Christina-

Taylor. But if it's really, really bad, just let her go and don't let her suffer. Take her; don't let her be in pain."

⁓

I face the seemingly impossible task of trying to express in words the loss of a child, the love we shared as a family, and the light my daughter added to the world.

The tragedy that ripped through Tucson that January Saturday in 2011 tore from us someone we'll never get back and changed our lives forever.

But though Christina-Taylor is gone, her memory will live on.

I don't expect to see John that morning, January 8, 2011, after he leaves to work with suppliers at our nearby rental house. When we reconnect, it will be for the worst reason any parent can imagine.

CHAPTER TWO

A LOVE STORY

TWO ARE BETTER THAN ONE,
BECAUSE THEY HAVE A GOOD REWARD FOR THEIR LABOR.
FOR IF THEY FALL, ONE WILL LIFT UP HIS COMPANION.
BUT WOE TO HIM WHO IS ALONE WHEN HE FALLS,
FOR HE HAS NO ONE TO HELP HIM UP (ECCLESIASTES 4:9–10).

To tell you about my beautiful girl, I must take you back to when I met the man I fell in love with and who would become her father. John Green and I met at the University of Arizona in 1990, and while it may not have been love at first sight, it was the beginning of something deeper and truer.

I was born October 1, 1965, in the Bronx. My father, a New Yorker named Richard Segalini, was a financial planner; my mother,

Yolanda Lopez, a Pan Am flight attendant from South Texas. My father had a successful career and traveled often, and they had met on an international flight.

My father's success afforded us a good life. After my younger brother Paul was born, we moved from New York City to a beautiful house in Scarsdale in Westchester County, New York. My dad commuted to work every day, and my mother stopped flying and devoted time to the Manhattan chapter of Pan Am's charity. She was also active in the PTA at our school after my youngest brother, Greg, was born.

Life was fun and exciting, and we had lots of room to run and play. We traveled a lot, but we rarely missed a Sunday dinner at my father's parents' house. Sundays were quintessentially Italian, filled with family, love, laughter, and of course tons of food.

My father's work required more and more international travel, and the time away took a toll on my parents' marriage. When I was about ten, my mother's doctor recommended a dryer climate for her allergies. We moved across the country to Tucson, closer to my grandmother Faustina, with whom I was very close. My Aunt Elida and Uncle Red Hildreth lived not far away too, and became like a second set of parents to me and my brothers.

Dad took a job in Zurich. He visited when he could for the next three or four years, but that simply didn't work. Mom was doing all the parenting and finally decided to make the split official when I was about fourteen.

I was heartbroken, because I had been close to my father until we moved away. Yet I felt bad for my mother, because she had tried everything to make it work. Divorce was not as common in the late seventies as it is now, and she didn't get the kind of support that a single mother might get today.

My mother did an amazing job making a life for me and my brothers. She was happier, and that made us happier. She worked part-time as a teacher in a private school, but her priority was to spend time with us. While we had clearly downsized from the lifestyle we had enjoyed in Scarsdale, we kids hardly noticed. We were close and life was good again.

My mother had an inner strength. She fought for what she cared about. Beautiful and poised, she had given up a lifestyle in New York to be happy and to make us happy. She showed us that to live where there is no love is not strength but weakness. She was amazing and loved me dearly, teaching me so much.

I enrolled at the University of Arizona in the fall of 1983 to study business. My hope was to become a financial planner like my dad, but it seemed everyone else in the family thought I should become a nurse. Maybe it was because I tended to be a nurturer, being the eldest daughter in a broken home. Though I often took care of my aging grandmother and looked after my brothers, I didn't see nursing in my future, at least back then.

While I wasn't much of a baseball fan, I had friends on the baseball team who were friends of John. He had been a pitcher at the University of Arizona and was now playing minor league ball in the Chicago Cubs organization. During the off-season he would come back to finish his engineering degree one semester at a time. When we met in 1990, we hit it off immediately as friends. He was a big, strong, athletic guy who had a good sense of humor, and we found it easy to talk. It also didn't hurt that he was handsome.

As our friendship grew, I learned that John had grown up in a traditional family, with both parents, a brother, and two sisters, in Wilmington, Delaware, outside of Philly. His mother, Sylvia, was a schoolteacher, and his parents virtually lived within the same twenty-mile radius their whole lives. He doesn't remember his father, Dallas Green, as a big-league pitcher, because John was a toddler at the time. But as he grew older he spent more and more time with his dad during his baseball career.

John would tell me stories of going to spring training with his dad almost every year, of being on the road with him a lot, of attending sometimes sixty-five big-league games a year. Even as a teenager, John had worked out with big-league teams, impressing the players with his work ethic. He wasn't just the manager's privileged son. He worked.

I heard about his high school and college pitching career, how he played junior college ball in Oklahoma, then in Chicago when his dad became general manager of the Cubs. He told me of the future big leaguers he played with and how he had back-to-back College World Series experiences in the early 1980s. He also told me of playing in the minors after that.

We began to see each other romantically after two years of friendship. It wasn't until later that I realized that our friendship had helped us build the foundation for what would be a solid marriage.

After being traded to the New York Yankees and reaching the triple-A level, John's baseball dream ended when he was released. That took John some time to get over, because he loved the game so dearly. But, being tenacious, he finished his degree and became an engineer.

By then I had fallen madly in love with him. He was generous, old-fashioned, spoke his mind, and had a strong, outgoing personality, much like myself. He was also a Christian, which was important to me, as my faith helps define who I am.

> *John: Roxanna has always had that untamed spirit about her, something that challenged me. I liked that about her. She's vivacious and spirited about things, and that struck me. Plus she was beautiful, with dark skin and long dark hair.*

After college I took a job selling life and health insurance and mutual funds, while John was working as an engineer. Though there were parts of my job I really liked, the dog-eat-dog nature of the business was getting to me. I began wondering whether my family was right. Maybe I was more cut out for something like nursing. I began looking at other options, including the medical career I had always dismissed.

I could see that John was getting restless with his job too and didn't really love what he was doing. He was volunteering as a scout for the Baltimore Orioles, a part-time thing where he would report to the big-league team on local high school baseball stars who might be candidates for recruitment. He talked often about how much he missed baseball. Finally the day came when he said he wanted to return to the game full-time.

I didn't know as much about baseball as I did about other sports, but I knew coaches and managers were rarely home. The instability of my childhood during my parents' divorce made me wary of John's return to baseball. When I asked in what capacity he saw himself, he said scouting. Everything he had learned from playing his whole life, growing up around the big leagues and playing in the minors, told him he could do this.

I knew this was his passion and his dream. Though I had fears of him being away and traveling a lot, I wanted to support him, because I feel that if you are happy with your career, you will flourish in life.

My mother's mother, Faustina, died in 1993 when I was twenty-eight, before she was able to see me marry and have children. She had been a wonderful model to me of what a grandmother should be, and I knew my mother would follow in her footsteps with my children when they came along. I had been so close to Faustina that I longed for the same grandmother-grandchild relationship for my kids.

As we got closer to marriage, John landed a job as area scout for the Baltimore Orioles, covering Colorado, Utah, New Mexico, and Arizona. That would require a move of a little more than a hundred miles north and made me realize it was time for me to get out of financial planning. I decided to go into nursing, a move I knew would make me happy. We married on New Year's Eve of 1994 and moved just south of Phoenix to Ahwatukee. We purchased our first home, agreed we were in no hurry to have children, and set about enjoying everything about married life. We had lots of friends who had moved to that area, so we socialized, I studied, he scouted, and life was good.

Over the years I would travel with John to every big-league park in the United States and gradually get to know all the people he had known since he was a kid. I became a baseball fan. It became a part of me and I found I really enjoyed it, learned a lot, and looked forward to every spring training and every summer—whether he was scouting high schoolers, college kids, or pros. There were sights to see and things to do in every town.

After a few years, John was promoted to eastern supervisor, which he handled from his parents' house in Pennsylvania while I finished nursing school. Of course I couldn't travel with him all the time, and the on-the-road lifestyle of a scout can be hard on a marriage. His typical workday started in the middle of the afternoon and ended in the wee hours, drinking and talking baseball with friends and coworkers. Then they sleep all morning and start the pattern all over again. I began to wonder what that kind of a schedule would mean to a family. One thing was sure: I at least needed to be living with John, not several states away.

The break we needed came when there was a shake-up in the Orioles' front office and John entertained offers from both the Cincinnati Reds and the Pittsburgh Pirates. He was close to a lot of the guys with the Pirates and respected them, so he chose the Pittsburgh job—which meant I could join him on the East Coast.

As soon as I finished nursing school, I was ready to go. Being from the East, it sounded like a great idea to get back there, and maybe now it was time to try to start a family.

I left everything I knew, and at first it didn't really matter where I was going to live. I was proud of John for getting the promotion, and as long as he and I were together, I knew that wherever we landed would be home. Our plan was to have two or three children, and as soon as they were old enough, we would all travel with John during the summers.

I was ready to settle in one place for a long period and become a stay-at-home mom for most of the year. John was happy, doing what he was born to do. Baseball is in his blood, part of who he is. I was looking forward to our new adventure.

We moved to Conowingo, Maryland, where we rented a 250-acre farm from John's parents. It was a beautiful place, but talk about remote! We had moved from a growing, bustling neighborhood to the middle of nowhere in the dead of winter, 1998.

During the first week there I discovered I was pregnant, and we were thrilled. But John immediately hit the road in his new role, and I have to admit it was hard to be alone in a new place and a new climate. I knew no one in Maryland except John's sister and brother-in-law, Dana and Mark Ressler, who lived on the same property. They were very busy people, but they were wonderful to me while John was gone.

My pregnancy turned out to be high risk, because during my fourth month I developed *placenta previa*, which causes hemorrhaging and requires complete bed rest. For the last five months of my pregnancy, I had to be on the couch or in bed reading or watching TV and could get up only to go to the bathroom. For a Type A personality, being deprived of all activity—even housework—was torture. Although I missed John dearly, I didn't want to burden him with the difficulties of my pregnancy. It was hard enough for him to be on the road for his job, and I didn't want him to worry.

All this was worth it because, come late summer, we were going to have a son. Now that was something to look forward to.

I have a typically busy Saturday morning planned, January 8, 2011. Pick up Dallas from a sleepover. Get him to karate. Get Christina-Taylor ready for a morning outing with a neighbor. But the day turns out anything but typical.

CHAPTER THREE

STARTING A FAMILY

THEREFORE I ASK THAT YOU DO NOT LOSE HEART AT MY
TRIBULATIONS FOR YOU, WHICH IS YOUR GLORY (EPHESIANS 3:13).

I was worried. Here it was, 1999, and I was pregnant with our first child, confined to bed on a remote farm while my husband traveled most of the time. I wasn't naïve to the temptations of the road, and while I trusted him, I also knew John enjoyed staying up all hours of the night drinking and talking baseball with his colleagues.

John: The fact is, I was drinking a fair amount, still doing the things I had done as a college and pro player. That was a test to our marriage. For five months of the year I was gone three weeks of every month. It was one thing when we didn't have kids and Roxanna could be with me a lot. But now she would have to run the house, raise our son, handle everything.

I had known from the beginning that a big-league baseball scout could be only as good as his wife. She had to be a champ and accept a difficult life. I grew up in a home where my mother had to raise four kids while my dad was gone much of the time.

But now I too had to uphold my end of the bargain. I had to resist the temptations of the road. I had seen colleagues of my dad go through three and four marriages because of their lifestyles, and now that was beginning to happen to my friends too. Roxanna had already been wounded by divorce in her own family. We certainly didn't want that. We loved each other and wanted our marriage to last a lifetime, but I have to admit, she finally had to put her foot down.

She told me, "I'm not sure this baseball thing is going to work out if this is the way it's going to go. We're about to start a family . . . "

"Leaving baseball is not an option," I said, "because this is what I'm going to do for a living. But I hear you. Family is first, then the job. And I'm willing to put everything else aside."

I meant it. And that's what I did. I quit drinking, and I even gave myself a curfew. I'd still go out with the guys after games, but there was no alcohol for me, a regular bedtime, and no hangovers in the morning. I wasn't a kid anymore. It was time to grow up.

~

John is a man of his word, and that really put my mind at ease. It helped too that he was so excited about soon having a son. I know he was envisioning teaching him everything he knew about baseball and maybe producing another Dallas Green.

That was the name we settled on too. John's dad is George Dallas and is known by his middle name. John's middle name is Dallas. So we would have the first Dallas Green whose real first name was Dallas. We liked the sound of Jordan, from the river in the Bible, for a middle name. And basketball great Michael Jordan was very popular at the time, which was a plus.

Spending so much time on the couch or in bed for more than the last half of the pregnancy allowed me a lot of time to read and think. My nursing training made me curious about early childhood development, and the more I read and thought about it, the more proactive I decided to become. It was hard enough for a social person like me to endure isolation and loneliness; I wasn't going to inflict that on my son.

I really looked forward to motherhood and decided I would take lemons and make lemonade. My mother was scheduled to come out and help me with the baby; but as soon as I recovered, I was going to get back out into the world. I would post flyers at the post office and at stores, announcing a playgroup for other mothers and babies. It would be great to meet other mothers and start finding little friends for my son.

Dallas arrived two weeks early on August 26, 1999, which was fine with me, and the delivery was easy, compared to the pregnancy. He was long and thin, a beautiful, dark-haired boy, and like any other mother, I was thrilled to hold him and make sure he was physically perfect. I'd had the typical fears of a first mom, worrying that something would go wrong or that he would have some defect.

I didn't want to invent problems, but I have to say I was troubled from the very beginning when I couldn't seem to connect with him. You don't expect much from newborns in the way of eye contact or their seeming to engage with you right away, but Dallas seriously seemed to be in his own world right from the start. He wasn't interested in breastfeeding, which was a big priority of mine. And while I was able to rationalize and push aside my fears the first day, telling myself I was imagining things, I couldn't do that for long.

I was coming up on my thirty-fourth birthday, was a nurse, and had plenty of friends who'd had babies, so it wasn't like I was a naïve young mom, even though Dallas was my first. Plus I had been doing all that reading over the last several months, so I had an idea what was going on.

By the time Dallas was three days old and I was at home with him and my mom, I knew there was something wrong with him. When your child doesn't eat, sleep, or poop right, red flags are flying everywhere. I had been hesitant to express my fears to anyone, but it didn't take long for my mother to notice too.

She had used natural childbirth with all three of us kids and had breastfed us, and I was determined to do the same. I kept calling my young country pediatrician and reporting to her on Dallas's difficulty feeding and sleeping, but she continually told me, "Just keep trying. Keep trying. He'll come around."

Finally, at three in the morning at the end of the third week, my mom and I looked at each other and I could see she knew too. "No more sleepless nights for you," she said. "He's not feeding; he's skinny as can be. Tomorrow I go out and buy bottles. Get over having to be the perfect mother. If it doesn't work, it doesn't work."

I felt like such a failure. I knew I had to get this kid gaining weight, but it was almost impossible to get him to even take a bottle. How was I supposed to get his digestive system to kick in if he wasn't eating as much as he needed?

My mother became a hero to me, sacrificing everything to do whatever needed to be done. I began seeing her as a Grandma Walton type, one who would do anything for her daughter and her grandson, forgetting about her own need for sleep.

We would hold Dallas and walk with him and rock him, and he would cry and cry. It was torture trying to get into him anywhere near the minimum amount of formula he needed every day. He would fall asleep during feeding, catnapping during the day but not sleeping at night. At wit's end, I would call my pediatrician and be told, "You need to sleep when your baby sleeps."

During the day, for a few minutes at a time?

When John would come home off the road he would be thrilled to see his son, and he would assure me the problems were just a stage. "Boys will be boys. He'll come around. He'll be all right."

But John wasn't up with him all hours of the night. I felt getting up with Dallas was my job, and I didn't want to add pressure to John's life.

John: It was really difficult at first, and I could see Roxanna was struggling. He wasn't eating right, he was fussy, he wouldn't sleep. I'm sure I was avoiding the issue, and maybe I didn't want to admit there was a real problem. I hoped it was a stage or at worst he was a slow developer, and I kept telling Roxanna he was going to be fine.

I'm pretty stubborn, but I am able to change my views when I finally see it or feel it. Unfortunately for Roxanna, I wasn't there yet. I wasn't on board.

My mother, bless her, stayed four weeks, and John wondered why I was crying as we drove back after dropping her at the airport. I didn't have the heart to tell him how rough it had been. I was sleep deprived with her there and helping; what would happen when I was on my own?

John and I had talked about having two or three children, but I was already rethinking that. What if we had another boy—they're more prone to autism-type issues—one with similar challenges? I just didn't know if I could cope.

I finally learned that the only way to get Dallas to sleep was by driving him around in the car. But I was a city girl and didn't like driving alone in the country, especially at night. Being dead tired myself and not wanting to wake him by taking him out of his car seat, when we would get back to the house I would often just sit with him in the car with the engine and heater running and fall asleep myself.

I would drag Dallas back and forth to the pediatrician, who kept telling me I was just missing my mother, or that I needed to hire help. My mom would learn stuff from TV or books or talking to her doctor friends and call with advice. She seemed the only one who believed me at first, telling me I didn't just need more help; I had a special needs child.

She came back for the holidays, which was a relief, and I went out to Arizona when I could. Then in late February she joined me so we could all go to spring training with John. The best thing Mom did was assure me I wasn't crazy.

As the months wore on, I tried everything. There was a program in the city where moms and kids could get involved in interactive music and games. I loved that, but it wasn't for Dallas. He didn't seem to like being with other kids. Noise bothered him. Too much activity bothered him. When we had playgroups or visited his cousin or went to a ballgame, he wasn't happy. He would have meltdowns and cry and scream, and he wasn't happy unless he could be at home alone with just me or sitting by himself lining up his toys. I kept taking him to the pediatrician, who simply didn't seem to get it. And, of course, whenever we were there, he would be on his best behavior. So I feared she thought I was the problem, an obsessive first-time mom losing her mind.

When I discovered I was pregnant again in early 2001, when Dallas was just over a year old, I nearly panicked, eager to know as soon as possible whether it was another boy. By then I had a pretty good idea what we were dealing with. Dallas was clearly somewhere on the autism spectrum. I was relieved to learn we were expecting a girl, though that certainly was no guarantee against autism.

We soon hired a nanny three days a week, an elderly woman named Nona, who turned out to be a saint. I wanted a local "grandma influence" on Dallas and for her to really get to know him and understand his problems before our daughter came along. I was worried to death Nona would quit on me because Dallas was so challenging, but she was great.

At first she didn't see what I was seeing either. She had raised six children and had taken care of all her grandchildren, and she'd say,

"He is fine; he's just like all American boys." On the one hand, I was glad he wasn't too much for her, but on the other, I didn't want her to be naïve either.

Nona didn't even know what autism was, so I gave her books to read and talked to her about it a lot.

Every day I silently pleaded with God that Nona would be okay with all the challenges. We felt so blessed to have her and so fortunate that she stayed on. While most people—once they'd endured some long days and nights with him—would have just said they were sorry and couldn't do this, she would sit and rock him for hours if that was what he needed.

As the time drew closer to September, when our baby girl was due, Dallas became more and more challenging. He was nearing two years old and was learning how to really express himself. I got all the advice I wanted and a lot I didn't. People who didn't understand just thought I should be tougher on him, discipline him more, ask more, expect more of him.

But I knew. And somehow, some way, somewhere, I was going to find the help we needed for Dallas. Just like a troublesome car that won't act up when you take it to a mechanic, he was still usually just docile when I took him to the pediatrician. The advice was always the same and seemed to point the finger at me. *Get more help. You miss your mom. This isn't that out of the ordinary.*

But finally, Dallas had a meltdown in the pediatrician's office. As he had done so often in public, at other people's homes, at playgroups, and even at home when he was overstimulated, the little guy just lost it.

Something set him off, whether too much talk or activity or too much attention directed his way, and he became desperate to get out of there. I tried to calm him, but he screamed and cried and thrashed. He'd had enough and needed to be home, in his own environment, with his own things.

Finally, finally, she saw what I had been trying to tell her since he had been born. There was nothing normal about this. This was beyond typical. He needed medical help. And I was going to stop at nothing to find solutions for my son.

"You see?" I said. "This is what he does with me every day. We can go somewhere and everything will be fine for a little while. But when he's had enough, when it's time for him to go, nothing will calm him down besides getting out of there."

It was as if a light came on in her head. "Maybe he'd qualify for early intervention."

I didn't even know what that was, but it sounded like heaven. It was something, anything. And I was going to dive in and find out everything I could about it.

John: I hadn't wanted to admit that whatever was wrong with Dallas might be a lifelong problem. But once I realized it was serious and I got on board—where Roxanna had been for a long time—we attacked this with gusto. Was it embarrassing? Sure, at first. For one thing, everybody has their own ideas about mental and psychological issues like autism. A broken bone is one thing. A malfunctioning brain is another. People don't understand.

But I'm so proud of Roxanna, how she led the way in this. Once we realized this was a serious issue, we learned every-thing we could about it. She got involved in the Autism Society, and she soon knew as much as any therapist about how to modify behavior and help Dallas along. And she taught me. That became our mission: to do whatever we had to do to make Dallas's life manageable.

Lots of so-called experts have conflicting views on how to approach this and what to do, but she would not allow anyone to deter her from what she knew. From that day to this, we have stuck to the ideas that were the best fit for Dallas.

~⌒

It turned out there was an early-intervention specialty school for kids a half hour from our house. I was very pregnant, frustrated, and exhausted. But it didn't matter. Help was out there, and I was going to take advantage of it. I drove him every day.

Meanwhile, John and I loved the idea that a daughter would really balance our family. But without Nona, I don't know whether I could have coped.

It is supposed to get into the sixties by mid-day Saturday, January 8, 2011, but Christina-Taylor will need a wrap, maybe a hoodie, for her morning outing. She will roll her eyes at my over-protectiveness, but how can I know she would need much, much more than that?

CHAPTER FOUR

9/11/01

Do not be overcome by evil, but overcome evil with good (Romans 12:21).

I love that *Christina* is a variation of *Christ* and an anagram of *Christian*, but actually I got the *tina* part from my maternal grandmother, Faustina. *Taylor* is John's mother's maiden name, so there are lots of Taylors in his life. But just like Dallas's middle name had a twofold origin—the River Jordan and Michael Jordan—it happens that I was always a big fan of Elizabeth Taylor too.

Our plan was to call her by her full, hyphenated name. Sure, we often shortened it, but I'd say more than half the time we referred to her as Christina-Taylor. And I still prefer that. She always did too, often correcting people who called her Christina.

She would prove to be such a good baby that I called her my "angel in the wind." With an autistic two-year-old and a newborn, I needed strength just to get through the day. She was so easy, she gave me that strength. As she got older I sometimes called her Noonie, just because I thought it was cute. John came to call her Bobcat, because she was tough and fearless and sometimes roared when she didn't get her way or was being competitive. Dallas called her Crust at first because he could not say Christina-Taylor and thought it was funny. She called him Dallas's at first because he told her so many times that all the toys were "Dallas's."

My obstetrician had been telling me I was going to have a big girl. That sounded all right to me, because size sounded like health. I had felt so bad for Dallas, taking only a few ounces at a time those first several weeks while I was trying to bulk him up, get his digestive system working, and get him to sleep. I prayed this girl would eat and sleep like a typical baby from the beginning.

Because my first pregnancy had been high risk, I'd had to be very careful with this one too. Fortunately it didn't require bed rest, because even with Nona's help, I had to be an active mother. When it became obvious how big Christina-Taylor was going to be, my OB-GYN recommended inducing. Besides the baby's size, we lived in the middle of nowhere, so scheduling the birth seemed a much better idea than hoping we could get to the hospital in time.

Inducing sounded fine, I thought, "but no C-section. I definitely don't want that."

My real preference was natural childbirth, maybe with a few painkillers as I'd had with Dallas. Inducing alone was a big step for me, but we all knew it was prudent. A C-section was out of the question.

"What if she's even bigger than I think?" the doctor said.

I shook my head. "No C-section."

"All right," she said. "Your call."

We agreed on September 10, 2001, right around midday, and she asked me to arrive at Christiana Hospital in Newark, Delaware, near the University of Delaware, before dawn. "That way we can get your IVs started and get Pitocin into your system long before delivery time." Pitocin is the inducing drug.

John and I left the farm at about five in the morning. I was eager.

I don't know what I was expecting—perhaps that the Pitocin would get things started quickly—but midday seemed to come and go quickly. It felt to me as if things were happening, and I felt ready to explode. But there was no move to get me into the delivery room, and those tending my monitor readouts and checking dilation kept saying, "This baby doesn't want to come yet."

Well, I wanted her to come. I was getting more uncomfortable by the minute. "She'll come when she's ready," someone told me. There was little comfort in that. I was hungry, exhausted, irritated, and in excruciating pain. There would be no more pregnancies for me, I decided. I just wanted to get on with this.

A girlfriend came to visit in the middle of the afternoon, thinking she was going to see my baby. All she saw was a sign on the door in big block letters that said DOUBLE PITOCIN. She knew what that meant. "Look at you," she said. "Wow. Oh, my gosh!"

A few other friends and family members were there with me for much of the evening, and I began fearing it was going to be a long night. I knew I was in trouble when the second shift changed since we had arrived.

One by one my visitors started saying their good-byes. "It doesn't look like you're having this baby tonight," they were saying, heading home to bed.

"Oh, yes I am," I'd say, not as sure as I sounded. I was determined, if that meant anything.

Sad to say, there's a reason some nurses are on night shift. As a nurse, I can say this: some have terrible bedside manners. And mine was one of those. As the clock crept toward midnight, only John and I were left in the labor room. He had stretched out on the visitor's bed, a tiny thing my big husband was giving the true test. The nurse bustled in and said, "You both might as well go to sleep." And then she was gone. What?!

That was all John needed to hear. It seemed I heard him snore in the next second, while all I was thinking was, *Hold on! I'm having this baby tonight. Soon!* Plus, how was I going to sleep in such pain, with all the drugs in me just about turning me inside out, wires attached, machines whirring and humming?

"John," I said. "Get up."

"Huh? Wha—?"

"You need to go out there and tell that nurse I need a C-section."

"No, now we've talked about this, Roxanna. You said you'd never—"

"I know what I said."

"You've been saying this since Dallas was born. No C-section unless it was really necessary."

"Well, now it's necessary. I can't take it anymore, John. Please."

He left and was soon followed back in by an associate of my doctor. She said, "Are you sure, Roxanna, because you've been clear all along on this . . . "

I'd been in hard labor for more than twelve hours. "This is not what I signed on for," I said. "Yes, this is what I want now."

"All right, let me check you one more time, and then we'll do what we have to do."

A minute later she said, "Guess what? This baby is ready to come."

An hour later—well after midnight—they laid across my chest a gorgeous almost nine-pound Christina-Taylor Green, olive skinned, brown-eyed, and dark haired. After a tough pregnancy and easy delivery of Dallas, I'd had an easy pregnancy and torturous birth of my girl. But all that was quickly forgotten. Our family was complete. The look on John's face alone made it all worth it.

I couldn't wait to introduce Christina-Taylor to Dallas. We had been preparing him for months, showing him Mommy's tummy, telling him his sister was in there. We had read him a book over and over about welcoming a new baby into the family. And we were prepared to shower him with attention and his own special gifts when people made a fuss over his sister and brought her things.

I was delivered to a regular room with a roommate who was sleeping in the bed near the window. Mine was near the door, and there was nowhere for John. I urged him to go to his parents' home nearby, where Dallas was, and he quickly took me up on it.

If anything, I was too exhausted to sleep. I still had a lot of drugs in my system, and, naturally, hospitals are not quiet or conducive to rest. Plus, every few hours they brought Christina-Taylor to me. Wiped out as I was, I couldn't get over her. She was plump and robust, engaged and aware.

John: Once I was sure the baby was fine, I was relieved to be able to go get some sleep. My parents' farm was in Pennsylvania, about forty minutes away. I collapsed onto the couch and slept until about 9:30 in the morning when my mother roused me.

"It looks like a small plane has hit one of the World Trade towers," she said.

I was groggy as we gathered around the TV. While we watched the second plane hit the other tower, and of course everybody knew immediately these were no accidents. I quickly called Roxanna, got ready, and took Dallas to the hospital to see his mom and meet his new sister.

I was desperate for some sleep that morning, but I heard people hurrying past my bed and to the bed of my roommate. She had her TV on low and they were whispering urgently, clearly trying not to disturb me but doing a good job of doing just that. I knew something big had to be happening on TV, so I turned mine on. Like everybody else in the world, at first I couldn't believe what I was seeing. But it wasn't a movie, not a documentary about something that might happen. Both World Trade Center towers had been hit, and it was hard not to feel as if we were in a war zone.

I kept pinching myself to be sure I wasn't asleep. In fact, I pinched myself so many times I left welts on my arm. How could this be happening at all, let alone on the same date my baby girl had been born? I couldn't remember ever having two such disparate emotions at the same time. I was thrilled with my new daughter and relieved after such a difficult delivery, yet I was horrified at what I was watching.

When John arrived I was amused at first by Dallas's reaction to Christina-Taylor. He had no interest! He didn't even want to look at her. John held him up to where he could see her on my chest, and he looked everywhere but at her.

As the news continued to pour in, we began to wonder what was to become of us, of everybody, of our country. Manhattan was only about 130 miles from the hospital. Not only did we hear of the attack on the Pentagon, a hundred miles away, and the plane crash in Pennsylvania 225 miles away, but rumors were also swirling of attacks on several other major cities. They proved false, of course, but for a while we wondered if the whole country was under attack.

Hospital personnel began asking for volunteers to give up their beds in the event they would need them for victims in the tri-state area. I was eager to get out of there, but it turned out I didn't have to leave. I stayed the required two days and was glad to finally be headed home. I recall kidding the nurse about changing the date on the birth certificate to the day before, but we both knew that wasn't happening.

> *John: At first I thought it was unfortunate—too bad that Christina-Taylor was born on a day that, like Pearl Harbor day, would forever live in infamy. But then I quickly moved to thinking that my daughter was one good thing that happened that day. Yes, people would always talk about it, and on the anniversary of the attacks it would be replayed over and over. But she could be a beacon of hope, an example of something good and pure, of something that went right on a horrible day.*

As soon as we got home I could tell Christina-Taylor was going to be a totally different baby. I didn't favor her over Dallas, of course, didn't love her more just because she was easier. I was determined to make plain to both of them what I felt deeply in my heart, that I cherished them both with a mother's love that is beyond description. They would have different needs, different strengths, different weaknesses. But they would get equal love and attention.

Because of Dallas's issues, he really communicated only at home. He didn't talk to other people, but he talked to me, and I could understand him. The fact was he had changed his tune from before Christina-Taylor was born to now. He had told us he understood that our family was going to be bigger and he would have a sister. Now he was the same as he had been when he first saw her. Zero interest. Didn't want to see her, deal with her, talk about her, play with her, anything. His look told me he wished we could take her back to where we got her.

I had him 90 percent potty trained. Now he totally regressed. Experts told me not to change him, to let him wallow in it. That might have been good advice for a typical child, but I couldn't do that. At least at first. Finally I followed their advice, and it was effective. Yet in many ways, I felt I had gotten him a step ahead and now he was three steps behind. Competition from a new sister was proving too much for him.

He was still having a terrible time sleeping. Whatever was happening in that little brain of his would not turn off just because it was bedtime, quiet, and the lights were off. When we'd check on him, he'd be wide awake, restless, and staring at the ceiling. I didn't know what to do. A two-year-old needs his sleep—and not just dozing off during the day.

I kept trying to get Dallas to warm up to Christina-Taylor and to engage with her. Usually he would just roll his eyes and run away.

She was probably not even two months old when we all flew to Puerto Rico with John on a scouting trip. That began a tradition of traveling and spending a lot of time together in hotel rooms. The kids were too young to sit through batting practice or a game, so often it was just the three of us together in the room or at the pool as John was out on assignment. Though Dallas was still indifferent to her or even antagonistic, whatever we did, it was just the three of us. So they had little choice but to eventually become close—playing games, reading, watching educational videos, whatever.

As Christina-Taylor got older and was able to crawl around and even start to walk, Dallas became even more exercised about her. It was important to him that his things were his things. There had to be rules and boundaries, and he had to be able to line up his toys just so. Nothing was worse than a precocious, roly-poly little girl upsetting his stuff.

Even a typical kid would be upset by losing his place as the star, the only one getting attention. But how much harder it had to be for a kid whose mind was different from others. He became agitated when we couldn't respond to him immediately because we were changing or feeding Christina-Taylor. I couldn't leave her on the floor alone with him if I had to run to the bathroom or take a phone call, because there was no guarantee he wouldn't bop her with his little plastic bat. He really didn't want her around.

We weren't the only baseball people who scheduled their children's births around the off-season. It was a great help to me that John was home for the first several months after Christina-Taylor was born. By now he was fully vested in doing what we needed to do for Dallas, and he was also more than willing to split the nighttime duties. If Dallas was fussy in the night, which he frequently was, or Christina-Taylor needed to be changed or fed, John did his part.

Luckily for us, Christina was a really happy child and already somehow knew how to wait and be patient. She was not high maintenance in the least, so it allowed us to juggle everything at once.

At least every other day, Nona helped take care of and entertain the kids during the day, and with John taking turns in the night, things were so much easier on me the second time around. And it became more and more fun as Christina-Taylor's unique, entertaining personality began to emerge.

Just over five weeks before January 8, 2011, a man I choose not to glorify or even name—he's had way more attention than he deserves—buys a box of Winchester bullets and a Glock 19 9-millimeter handgun with an extended ammunition magazine that holds thirty-three rounds.

CHAPTER FIVE

SOMETHING SPECIAL

ASK, AND IT WILL BE GIVEN TO YOU; SEEK, AND YOU WILL
FIND; KNOCK, AND IT WILL BE OPENED TO YOU. FOR EVERYONE
WHO ASKS RECEIVES, AND HE WHO SEEKS FINDS, AND TO
HIM WHO KNOCKS IT WILL BE OPENED (MATTHEW 7:7-8).

In January of 2003, we moved across the state line into Chester County, Pennsylvania, to the borough of West Grove, where John had been raised. I liked it because we moved into a development of big homes with lots of space, yet without the isolation of the old farm. Our house sat on a cul-de-sac in a nice neighborhood on a great lot backed by acres and acres. Ironically, John's parents moved to Maryland then, but they were still close enough. His sister Dana was only thirty minutes away. I soon discovered new friends and neighbors who really became helpful, so it couldn't have been better.

Another advantage was that since Dallas had been accepted and was going every day to the early-intervention school in Maryland, he automatically qualified for the Pennsylvania one. And it was much closer to our new house than the other had been to the farm. Where I spent a half hour each way getting him to and from the school in Maryland, this one took just a few minutes a day.

Now if I could just get my kids to act like brother and sister. Cute and sweet and dark and plump, sixteen-month-old Christina-Taylor was happy and seemed easily entertained. It was clear she was curious, but that didn't motivate her enough to move much yet. She loved to just sit and let people bring her stuff. She was a late walker and wouldn't start for another couple of months.

That suited Dallas, who was happy to have her stay clear of his toys. When I had to leave the room, however, I always took her with me, worried what he might do to her with that little plastic bat of his. Maybe he didn't like the cheerful noises she made. Maybe he was still just being rebellious. I didn't know, but I didn't trust them alone yet. As much as we worked on giving them equal time and attention, he was plainly jealous of her.

I began noticing that Christina-Taylor was becoming a ham. She loved the attention when she sang for us, so she'd sing more and more. She tried to dance in her own way too, to our delight. And once she figured out what Dallas's little plastic bat was for, she would smack a little ball all over the place. That young and already athletic! She already looked like a natural with that bat.

What impressed me even more, despite how young she was, was what I can describe only as an unusual maturity. We had therapists in and out of the house all the time for Dallas, and Christina-Taylor seemed to be figuring out that something different was going on, something special. As much as I tried to protect her from his frequent meltdowns, that wasn't always possible. She was often along when we would be playing with other kids at a park or somewhere else in public. If he was inappropriate, sometimes other parents would tell me in no uncertain terms what I ought to be doing about it. Or they would hurt my feelings by just grabbing their kids and leaving. Sometimes I explained the problem; sometimes I didn't. Often I just got him out of there.

As young as she was, I believe Christina-Taylor was learning that people are different and shouldn't be treated badly just because they are. In as simple a way as she could understand, I told her that we had to be aware of other kids who were different and that it was okay. "We don't make fun of them. We help them out."

My life still seemed an endless stream of trying to get real help for Dallas, hardly sleeping, and trying to convince John how serious the problem was. He couldn't deny any more that there were issues, but he was a long way from being willing to admit that to anyone else. Maybe he still had a dream that Dallas would follow in his and his grandfather's footsteps and be a big leaguer some day. Maybe he was just old school, having been raised in a household with four perfectly healthy kids. He was helpful; I'll say that. He'd come off the road and immediately take Dallas with him on the tractor to give me some downtime with just Christina-Taylor. He supported me and knew I was fighting for Dallas, but he was still embarrassed to let anyone know he had a son with special needs. Sometimes he would even downplay the problem with professionals who could have helped us more if they had known the extent of the problem. I would often have to appeal their decisions, ones they made because John and I weren't entirely on the same page yet.

Dallas was still having trouble sleeping. It seemed every time we checked on him, he was awake. That left him in bad moods during the day, sleepy all the time. Just like us.

⁓

A woman named Christine Naman, who had had a son born on September 11, 2001, came up with the idea for a book. She chose a 9/11 baby from every state and compiled a book of pictures called *Faces of Hope*. Christina-Taylor was chosen from the state of Maryland and had to have her picture taken for the book. We were invited to New York City for a photo session and a second birthday party for all the kids.

I could already tell Christina-Taylor was unusual because of the way she rolled with the punches with Dallas. She didn't get hurt, didn't get mad, and didn't cry, no matter how he treated her or ignored her. She just kept trying. She was strong. But I was really impressed by how she seemed to pick up on what a big deal this New York trip was. She loved posing for her picture, and she saw me consulting her godparents as well as Dallas's (Mary Jo Smith and her husband, Roy, who John knew from the Pirates) about the perfect dress for her for the occasion. Mary Jo is the one who found the red, white, and blue dress Christina-Taylor would wear to New York.

I had to find the right dress for me too, and my mother came out to join us for the New York trip, so Christina, even at two, caught on quickly that this was something special—and so was she. The five of us enjoyed the weekend, and she loved being the center of attention. Of course the *Faces of Hope* children were too young to understand the true significance of the day. They were surrounded by cameras all weekend, appeared on TV shows, went on a boat tour, and Toys"R"Us even shut down for just the kids.

It would be several years before Christina-Taylor understood the gravity of 9/11. While she was young, she just knew that for some reason it was like a national holiday. Under her photo in *Faces of Hope* was this: *I hope you know all the words to the national anthem and sing it with your hand over your heart.*

I hope you jump in rain puddles.

Soon two very significant events occurred in the life of our family, and both of them gave more evidence that we were raising a very special little girl.

For two years, Dallas had virtually pretended that Christina-Taylor didn't exist, or if she did, she was a nuisance. Naturally that was a big concern for us. Here we had this beautiful little family, but we longed to have our kids enjoy each other and become buddies.

Christina-Taylor seemed to adore her brother, and she just would not be put off no matter how he treated her. While it had taken her a little extra time to start walking, very early on it had become apparent that she had an advanced vocabulary, sense of humor, and even maturity level. She didn't act like any two-year-old I had ever seen.

Now she was running and jumping and entertaining us all, even making Dallas smile. I don't remember a specific incident or exactly when it happened, but it was as if someone flipped Dallas's switch. He couldn't have missed that Christina-Taylor delighted us as much as he did, that she was fun and mischievous and happy. Maybe he decided that if he couldn't beat us, or her, he'd join us and become a fan of hers too.

Overnight it seemed that Dallas decided, *Okay, she is fun, she can be a great playmate, and we are going to be friends.* It was as dramatic and thorough a change in attitude as John and I could imagine. Dallas wasn't just tolerating her. He loved her and included her, and they became best friends.

Dallas was still deeply challenged by his autism, so it was great to have at least one little person he enjoyed interacting with. They still squabbled occasionally, as kids will do, but they were close. He still had terrible sleep habits and was up all hours of the night, something that indicated to me that Asperger's Syndrome had to be part of his autism package.

Christina, on the other hand, loved to sleep, especially in our new Pennsylvania house. How those two kids could get along so well and play together so long every day and then have opposite experiences at bedtime puzzled us to no end. We were on the verge of asking Dallas's doctor to put him on a sleep aid—something I had resisted for years—when John came up with an idea.

Dallas slept, or tried to sleep, in a double bed. Meanwhile, Christina-Taylor was snoozing away in her own room, cheerfully exhausted from the day. Whether John thought Dallas could benefit from a model sleeper like Christina or simply knew that she would be a calming influence on him, I don't know. But one night we put Christina in Dallas's bed. To our surprise and relief, he didn't keep her up. She fell right to sleep. And when we checked on him later, Dallas was sound asleep too. Within a few nights he was going to bed at a reasonable time and sleeping through the night.

What a welcome change that was for all of us! Sleep benefits everybody, and our not having to get up with him in the night made us feel so much better. Dallas became a different kid, not being so sleepy during the day, and we began to see real progress.

From that point on, family life became different for all of us. Dallas still had significant challenges, but as a unit, we started to have a lot of fun together. We traveled with John when we could—even to spring training, and we became a real team. When he had to be on the road without us, the kids looked forward to his getting back all the time. They would hear the garage door and squeal, "Daddy's home!" and run to him.

Whenever we were on the road, I worried about Christina-Taylor because she was absolutely fearless. She would try everything and do anything.

~⌒~

I was glad to have Dallas in early intervention because they concentrated on special activities, and I began to see small improvements. Things weren't happening fast enough to suit me, though, and I would describe his progress as baby steps.

Pennsylvania officials would visit us and various therapists would evaluate Dallas and conclude that he would never go to regular school but would wind up in some special school in Philadelphia. Frankly, that made me angry. I didn't want to believe it, and I wasn't going to have that. I believed that if I worked hard enough with him, I would be able to help him. He would be able to stay in the early-intervention program or maybe go to special ed classes at a typical school. My ultimate dream was of him eventually being integrated into a regular class at a traditional school.

I didn't reveal my anger to the experts, but as soon as they left I would rip up whatever brochures they had left for me. I knew they were just doing their jobs and giving me the best advice they could. But I was fighting it. That was not going to happen to this family, to my son. There had to be a better way. I would never give up. I had poster board on which I listed all the possibilities for Dallas. I would Velcro on the name of one approach or treatment, and if it didn't work, I'd rip it off and attach another. Trial and error became virtually my full-time job.

Our biggest break came when a Pennsylvania state psychologist finally spent a lot of time with us and carefully studied Dallas, now five years old. In the past, whoever had been there was around only a short time and jumped to conclusions based on limited access. They would tell me that boys will be boys, that all kids have different timetables and milestones, that he was still young and would come around, all that.

I'd heard it all before, but nothing was helping. I wanted him diagnosed so he would qualify for all the help he needed. I can't tell you the number of times I discovered a program I thought would be helpful only to be told, "Sorry, your son doesn't qualify for that."

How would he qualify? By being diagnosed with autism.

Where some parents—and John admits he was one—resist a kid being labeled because of the long-term stigma that can result, my reading had told me that the right diagnosis would open doors for Dallas. I had read everything there was to read on the subject, and I knew that if you aren't proactive when your child is young, you can never go back. I didn't want Dallas turning six, seven, eight, or even ten and beyond without some kind of more aggressive formal treatment.

Well, this psychologist determined that Dallas had a little bit of this and a little bit of that, all fitting on the autism spectrum, but including Asperger's and ADHD, among other things. "Maybe it doesn't perfectly fit the definition," he told me, "but I'm going to write *autism*, because you guys need help. And this will accomplish that."

As a nurse, I was happy. I'd much rather know what we're facing than not. Finally, I saw a light at the end of the tunnel. Even if I'd rather have heard that he was perfectly normal, I knew better and finally knew what we were dealing with.

John was devastated. For a long time he wouldn't tell people that Dallas had autism. He wouldn't lie. He just wouldn't mention it. To his credit, John would talk with me about it. And hard as it was for him to have his son "labeled," as he called it, he eventually heard me. I'd say, "John, this is what it is, and I don't care what people think. We have to get him help."

Once he realized I was right and that any embarrassment over having something other than a perfect kid was misplaced, John became a true ally and we became one in the effort. Progress would be slow but sure over the years, and John has been able to teach Dallas certain manly social skills—a firm handshake, looking a person in the eyes, encouraging him to interact with people. He also taught him baseball, at which he has excelled. Whether an autistic child could ever reach the top levels of the game is yet to be seen, but Dallas has done well for his age.

Best of all, finally having a diagnosis did open those doors and get Dallas the right services and treatment. The state had previously avoided providing those at all costs, because it's an expensive undertaking. It requires a lot of resources for not only the child, but also for the family. But now they welcomed Dallas as a bona fide candidate for treatment, and we never looked back. He's now in a traditional class in a typical middle school, and the fabulous one-on-one aide who was assigned him years ago now serves the whole class. Praise God!

At 4:12 a.m., Saturday, January 8, 2011, the shooter is restless. He has been out running errands in the wee hours. He posts a message on My Space titled "Goodbye Friends."

CHAPTER SIX

AN EVEN BIGGER MOVE

[BE] CONFIDENT OF THIS VERY THING, THAT
HE WHO HAS BEGUN A GOOD WORK IN YOU
WILL COMPLETE IT UNTIL THE DAY OF
JESUS CHRIST (PHILIPPIANS 1:6).

When she was three, Christina-Taylor started attending the best Christian preschool I could find. The next year, because her birthday just missed the kindergarten cutoff date, I sent her to a special prekindergarten Quaker school with a couple of her friends.

School really made Christina-Taylor come alive. She loved everything about it, had lots of friends, and got involved in all sorts of activities. She especially loved ballet at an early age, and that was where the ham in her really came out. She loved to be on stage, to entertain, to show off. Christina-Taylor was Miss Personality.

She got her independence and strong will from both John and me, and I like to think she got the entertainment gene from her dancing mother.

All during our four and a half years in Pennsylvania, John was traveling, we were going with him when we could, the kids were getting closer and closer, and life was good. We still had our share of challenges, of course. I liked that Dallas and Christina-Taylor squabbled like typical kids but also figured out ways to resolve their differences without our having to referee all the time.

> *John:* *Because of the industry I'm in, I didn't see the kids a lot in the spring. But they learned to take care of each other a little to give Roxanna a break. When we did travel together in the summer and fall, they could be just as at home whale watching in Cape Cod or frolicking in the hotel pool in Orlando or picking berries on the farm in Maryland as they were in Pennsylvania. They developed a unique relationship, and you could see it even in their body language. They truly cared for each other and could sit and talk together for hours.*
>
> *My being on the road so much was difficult, but Roxanna and I did some pretty good planning—having both kids born during my off-season, for one.*
>
> *Still, I missed a lot. I missed some of Christina-Taylor's dance performances, some of Dallas's programs and projects. I missed just being around my wife every day, the way most men get to be with their wives. When I knew she was under*

the weather but still had to handle everything at home, and I couldn't get back from wherever I was—that wears on you.

But there were good things about our life too, mostly that quality time we got to spend together in the summer and fall when my schedule eased up. Your life is what you make of it, and we determined to travel and do a lot of things together. For many years I was able to take either Dallas or Christina-Taylor, or both, with me just about wherever and whenever I wanted. And in the off-season, I was really home, at their beck and call.

That gave Roxanna a little break. A family can make things work for them if they structure it intentionally. And that's what we tried to do.

Christina-Taylor soon developed into quite the little diplomat. I would tell her to do something, clean up, straighten a room, whatever, and then I would overhear her negotiating with Dallas. She'd tell him Mom wanted him to do the work, and if he squawked, she'd promise to do something for him later.

As she began to grow up, her interests seemed to explode. She got involved in T-ball, soccer, and dancing. She loved animals and would even later talk about becoming a veterinarian some day.

No matter where our trips took us, I had to constantly be on guard. I worried about her, fearing something would happen. She ran everywhere, climbed everything, jumped over anything, swam too far, dove too deep, you name it. It was sure better than the alternative. I didn't want a girl who was afraid of everything or not interested in trying new things. Christina-Taylor was certainly the opposite of that.

As well as things were going in Pennsylvania, I missed my mother and my aunt and uncle, Elida and Red. Mom visited us a lot, but she wasn't getting any younger. One of my brothers was in Tucson and the other was farther west, in California, so I felt pretty far removed from them. We all saw each other only a couple or three times a year because of the distance and work schedules. Besides that, I also missed the warm weather. I told John that if it was at all possible, I'd love to move back to Arizona.

> *John:* My parents were pretty mobile, plus we knew we could always come back in the summers and see them. Roxanna had sacrificed a lot coming east with me so I could do what I had to do for my job. But I had been with the Pirates a lot of years by now, and they offered me the job of running their West Coast scouting operation. That meant we could move back to Tucson the following July.
>
> That would be great for the kids, to have a more steady influence from the other side of our family. Roxanna's mom, Yolanda, was in her seventies already, and Red and Elida were even older and their health was failing. It was time.

With a little less than a year to go before we headed back to Arizona, we celebrated Christina-Taylor's fifth birthday in September of 2006. Knowing this was going to be the last big party we would be able to throw for her out east with all her friends, we hosted a huge Hawaiian-style blowout, and my mother flew out for the festivities.

Christina-Taylor always liked to wear red, white, and blue on her special day, but this time she was old enough to start catching on to the significance of the date. Because it was also the fifth anniversary of the terrorist attacks, the media coverage was more intense than ever. I recall Christina-Taylor coming in and out of where we would be watching the retrospectives on TV and seeming to realize that 9/11 was anything but a holiday. When she was younger, starting with the weekend birthday activities in New York surrounding the release of the *Faces of Hope* book, I think she thought it was quite a coincidence that her birthday fell on such an important day. Now she was beginning to get the picture that something horrific had happened the day she was born.

When we began to talk in front of the kids about moving back to Arizona the next summer, neither of them was too thrilled about going. Obviously they were at impressionable ages, and most of their memories were from the Pennsylvania house. They had friends and classmates and schedules they were used to. Plus, for some reason, Christina-Taylor had gotten it into her head that she was destined to one day attend Penn State. I don't know if she had just heard us or other adults talk about the place, but her plan was to stay so she could go there. I have to admit we were amused by such a young girl talking about college and knowing exactly where she wanted to attend.

Fortunately we had several months to get Dallas and Christina-Taylor used to the idea of the move. We told them they would be going to the same school, riding the same bus, and that we would live within five minutes of Grandma so they would get to see her every day. Best of all, we would have a pool.

"Well, okay," Christina-Taylor said finally. "But when I'm old enough, I'm still going back to go to Penn State."

⁓

We closed on our new home in Tucson in late July of 2007. Dallas was about to turn eight and Christina-Taylor six. He had made such progress that we were thrilled that they would both be attending Mesa Verde Elementary and riding the school bus together. In fact, we discovered, they were the only two children at their stop. They were already best friends, but going to school together every day and playing together just solidified it. And though it might seem strange since Christina-Taylor was two years younger than Dallas, it was clear she was watching out for her brother too.

One of my favorite stories from that time came from Dallas's teacher, Bethany Papajohn, who has become a family friend. She tells me she remembers Christina-Taylor's and Dallas's first day at Mesa Verde. John and I took the kids first to Dallas's second grade class before the first bell and explored the room. Once he was settled in, we took Christina-Taylor to her kindergarten room.

Dallas's teacher told us that for the first hour of the day, Dallas kept asking about his sister and wondering where her room was and whether she was okay. "As soon as I got a break, I took him to her room so he could check in on her," Bethany said. "He was so pleased when he saw her in there, happy and playing. They hugged and then he and I went back to our room. As the morning went on, Dallas kept asking when recess was so he could check on her again.

When recess finally came, he and Christina-Taylor quickly found each other, hugged again, and went off to play together.

"Christina-Taylor pulled me aside later in the recess and asked me in all seriousness, 'How is Dallas doing? Is he behaving himself?' I assured her he was and that he was a wonderful boy and student.

"This recess scenario played out the same for the rest of the year. Christina-Taylor's teacher told me that Dallas often came to her and asked how his sister was doing. Their sweet, caring relationship was so obvious, as was the love they shared. You and John have done a beautiful job raising two loving and caring children."

Our church, the same one I had grown up in, was just around the corner from my mother's house—where we stayed for the first four weeks while we were having a lot of renovation done on our new place. But even after we moved in, after Sunday school each week, Grandma would have the children over to her house to play and sometimes take them to a nearby park. Dallas was still very much in his own world and content to play alone or with Christina-Taylor. But she immediately began to soak up my mother's personality and views. The two of them even prepared Sunday dinner together often.

Grandma was with the kids at least three or four days a week, helping drive if one had to go one way and the other somewhere else. It was so good to have that influence on both kids, but in many ways Christina-Taylor became a little clone of my mother. She loved being outside with her in the garden. And when my mother gave her a miniature pink Singer sewing machine, Christina got real excited about learning to sew.

Grandma was also still very athletic, though she was slowing down. She would take the kids to play tennis, having excelled at it herself years before. And she loved music. Christina-Taylor enjoyed playing my mother's grand piano and even dancing around with her. It wasn't long before Christina even started asking for a guitar, which we would get for her for Christmas a few years later.

Best of all, my mother looked forward to things like grandparents' day at school, the book fair, or any program the kids were involved in. She was an active volunteer at their school too. You couldn't have asked for a more involved grandmother.

My mother had always been an active, caring, sensitive, giving person. She believed in doing things for the less fortunate, in standing up for things you believed in, in involving yourself in political and humanitarian causes. I knew that about her from my childhood, when she was so busy with Pan Am's Manhattan-based charity. I also recalled that she had been active in political campaigns when I was a kid. Now I was seeing the same traits in Christina-Taylor. She also got a lot of that from me, but naturally I had been influenced by her grandmother too.

After all the time they spent together, talking about why getting involved in politics was important and even going to fundraisers and events together, it shouldn't have surprised me that Christina-Taylor came to recognize the names of local candidates. She would see me watching the local news coverage, and even at that age ask who I was for and why. It was very unusual for a kid her age. She used phrases I knew she had gotten from my mom and would say things like, "I want to be involved in my community. I want to learn about government. I want to help."

When I asked why, she would say, "It's interesting. And fun!"

Who could know that an innocuous message I sent would one day change our lives forever?

We had bought a home in an older neighborhood with beautiful, well-kept homes and a largely mature population who seemed to enjoy their privacy and quiet. The first thing I wanted was to redo the flooring in our house, which meant a lot of activity, trucks in and out, a dumpster set up out front, the whole works.

I got a directory of the neighborhood for a half a mile or so around and sent out a mailing, introducing our family and telling our neighbors what we were doing. I was basically assuring people that the dumpster and all the noisy activity was temporary. But I was also hoping that some might respond so we could get acquainted when we finally moved in from my mother's place.

One of the first replies I got was from a woman named Suzi Hileman, who lived with her husband Bill about half a mile away. She welcomed us to the neighborhood and, among other things, asked if we were sports fans. Were we ever! I wrote back to tell her of John's role with the Pirates and that I too enjoyed watching lots of sports. There aren't too many women who do, but Suzi and I immediately had that in common. She invited our whole family over to watch a game. It was a pleasant evening where we learned that the handsome couple in their fifties had been retired for several years and had a couple of grown kids in other parts of the country. Bill had been a broker for Goldman Sachs and had apparently done well enough that he had been able to retire before he turned fifty. They had moved to Tucson in 2006 from Marin County, California.

To Dallas's delight, even though Suzi wasn't yet a grandmother, she kept a box of toy dinosaurs and Legos in the house. While he was captivated by those, Suzi taught Christina-Taylor to play pick-up sticks. We all seemed to hit it off, despite the differences in our ages.

When the Hilemans went on vacation, they would pay Christina-Taylor a few dollars to water their plants each day. Dallas and I would tag along, with me pretending to help but really just making sure everything was okay and that the water wasn't left on.

Christina loved that little job, because it was her first outside of chores at home, and she liked getting a little money. And once, on her birthday, Suzi helped her make business cards so she could start her own business of taking care of people's pets and watering their plants while they were gone. Suzi also took the kids to the zoo, and we visited the Hilemans now and then.

Like I say, that new acquaintance and neighborly connection just seemed interesting back then. No one knew what it would mean to our future.

Over the next three years, Christina-Taylor blossomed into the happiest, most precious girl I could imagine. I know all mothers think their kids are great, and I'm not pretending she was perfect. She could be obstinate, and she definitely wanted her own way. But one of my fondest memories of her last years with us was that she seemed constantly happy. She was a delight to be around.

She had picked up right where she left off as a precocious pre-schooler and soon became a straight-A student. She even talked about knowing how competitive the world was and that if she wanted to succeed, she'd have to graduate from a good college. If anything, she was interested in everything. That's no exaggeration. Whatever struck her fancy, she dived into it with everything that was in her.

Every day when she got off the bus and hurried into the house for a snack, she gave me a hug and a kiss and told me about her day, her activities, her friends, everything. She loved school, and I never had to nag her about getting her homework done. Our rule was that schoolwork had to be done before playing or doing sports, and she had no problem with that.

Besides ballet she also got interested in hip-hop, and it wasn't unusual for John to come home and find both of us dancing away. She loved animals, horseback riding, soccer, even gymnastics. Frankly, I tried to steer her away from that, as it was obvious she was not going to be petite. She didn't care. It was a sport and she was athletic, so she was going to give it a try.

My mother continued to have a huge influence on her. Besides being active politically, Mom volunteered to work in soup kitchens and engaged in fundraisers for the needy, and Christina tagged along and caught that bug too. It wasn't long before she was organizing food and clothing drives at school.

When Dallas and Christina-Taylor were eight and six, I went back to work as a home care nurse, so my mother did a lot of babysitting. During the U.S. presidential campaign of 2008, Grandma did a lot of fundraising and campaigning for Barack Obama—which caused a little humorous tension in our home, because John is a Republican.

Of course the Republican candidate, John McCain, was from Arizona, and the more involved my mother got, the more Christina-

Taylor got involved and the more questions she asked at home. It soon became clear that she was as curious about national politics as she had been about the local scene. I could hardly believe a girl that young could understand or care, but it was obvious she did. While other kids her age and older ignored news programs, she wanted to watch whenever we did, and she actually became conversant about the issues and even watched the debates.

My brother Paul, Christina-Taylor's godfather, tells this story:

It was early fall of 2008, and the presidential debates were underway; everyone in the country was talking about the upcoming election. Roxanna and Christina visited us here in Oakland, and we went to Piedmont Avenue (a well-known shopping district) to sightsee and shop.

Some Obama supporters had set up a table and had a bumper sticker that read, "Stop the Drama, Vote Obama."

Christina turned to me. "What does that mean, Uncle Paul?" She knew Grandma Segalini was a big Obama supporter, yet other members of the family—including her dad—were supporters of John McCain.

I gave her my opinion, saying the bumper sticker meant to call the current administration's policies drama because they had created strife for Americans at home with our economy and overseas with the wars. Of course, that's a heady topic, especially for an eight-year-old, but I could see in Christina's eyes and by her questions that she was at least getting the point that casting your vote for President was not a matter to be taken lightly. We talked about both candidates.

Finally I asked her who she would vote for. She paused and said she still needed to think about it. I said, "It is a tough decision as both men are great Americans, and it's not an easy job to be President."

That night after dinner, Christina told me she had made a decision. "We should stop the drama and vote Obama."

⟶

Christina-Taylor was also still loyal to the East Coast. She often told people she was from there and would be going back there. She would mention Penn State, but after traveling with us each year to Cape Cod, she got a taste of Connecticut and New York and would add that maybe she would choose NYU or "a school in Boston, because they have some fine ones there." If that sounds like she was mimicking adults, she was. She loved being with older people and wasn't afraid to insert herself into adult conversations. And she seemed to hear and soak up everything.

⟶

In the winter of 2008, John's ten-year run with the Pittsburgh Pirates came to an end, and he accepted a job with the Los Angeles Dodgers. That allowed us to stay in Tucson.

On February 1, 2009, we went to a party to watch that year's Super Bowl between the Pittsburgh Steelers and the Arizona Cardinals. Of course everyone in Tucson seemed to be rooting for the Cardinals. Except Christina-Taylor. "I'm from Pennsylvania," she announced. "I know the Steelers are going to win." I grimaced, but despite good-natured booing and jeering, she was right.

As advanced as Christina-Taylor was for her age, she was still just a seven-year-old after all. Occasionally her youth and naïveté would surface. While we were at a Washington Nationals baseball game in D.C. later that year, she had suggested to John and me that we should invite President and Mrs. Obama to the game so they could enjoy the great seats we had.

She said it as if it was as common as inviting friends or neighbors, which made John and me chuckle. "They're very busy," I said, "and so that is probably not going to be something we can do."

"But I know I would like the girls. I want to meet them."

The next day, when we were touring the capital, we took Christina-Taylor's picture outside one of the White House gates. "Why can't we go in and meet the Obamas?" she said. "I want to show them my campaign pin."

John explained that you don't just drop in on the President and his family.

She said, "Well, maybe next year we can invite them to a game."

John glanced at me, suppressing a smile, and said, "Okay, Christina, we will. Next year we'll invite them and see if they can come."

Being a loyal little Democrat by now, Christina-Taylor was mesmerized by all the retrospectives and the pomp surrounding the death and funeral of Senator Ted Kennedy on August 29, 2009. The TV coverage lasted all day, and I'll never forget her watching the whole thing with me and asking a lot of questions.

She was just a couple of weeks from her eighth birthday, but in many ways she seemed like an adult that day—even saying that someday she might want to be a senator. In other ways, she acted her age. Impressed by the pageantry, she said, "Mom, when you die, I'm going to have a funeral like that for you."

I laughed. "Christina, he was very famous and very wealthy, so I'm not going to have a funeral like that."

"Oh, but I will have one for you."

I could only smile. Surely no one in our little family would ever have a large funeral that attracted the attention of the whole nation, including the president.

Between 6:12 and 7:27 a.m., Saturday, January 8, 2011, the shooter makes various purchases and finally acquires a backpack-style diaper bag at a Super Walmart in Marana, Arizona.

CHAPTER SEVEN

FIRST LOSS

FOR TO ME, TO LIVE IS CHRIST, AND TO
DIE IS GAIN (PHILIPPIANS 1:21).

Christina-Taylor hadn't played baseball since T-ball back in Pennsylvania, but she loved tagging along with her dad when he was practicing with Dallas or assistant coaching Dallas's Canyon Del Oro Little League team. It soon became another obsession for her. No other sisters wanted to show up and shag balls during their brothers' practices and workout sessions. But she impressed John right away with how she could throw and even hit.

I knew she was a natural hitter from what she used to do with the toy bat, but I assumed she would rather play soccer with her girlfriends. When she started talking about wanting to play Little League in the summer of 2009, I cautioned her.

"You know," I said, "you'll probably be the only girl on the team. If you're lucky there might be one other."

"That's all right," she said. "I don't care about that."

She was independent and strong, confident enough that she didn't need to be on a team her friends were on. I know it made John happy, his whole life being baseball. And I knew she would take her competitive edge into this new pursuit. She already wanted to win at whatever she did, whether shooting baskets, swimming across the pool, running—it didn't matter.

Christina-Taylor was funny, a jokester, and a ringleader. Once she was singing from her second base position for her team, the Pirates, even during a play when she threw somebody out at first, and two of the other players were singing right along with her.

One coach told us that Christina spent several days negotiating the rules of a race between players and coaches, the prize being ice cream. The players got to run across the field frontward; the coaches had to run backward. Guess who won?

She was fun to watch. She liked second base best, but she also pitched.

> *John: I was the assistant coach, and of course my background was in pitching, but I had to bite my tongue and not coach her during the game unless she looked to me for help. She could throw strikes to me in practice, but at first she was a little afraid of hitting the batter. I told her not to worry about him, that she couldn't seriously hurt him anyway. "Just throw to the glove," I'd tell her, and otherwise I tried to keep my opinions to myself.*

In this league they have a rule that allows the hitter to decide whether they want to keep batting or take their base if they're hit by a pitch. Once when Christina-Taylor was hit, she insisted on staying in and hitting, and she drove in two runs. She was the RBI leader for her team. I couldn't believe how far she could hit a ball, and with regularity. To make the jump into kid-pitching competition, as opposed to T-ball or coach-pitch, and do as well as she did, well, I was proud.

One of the best parts of this was that she and I were able to take our baseball conversations to a different level. I didn't want to push her just because I was a baseball man, but she really wanted to learn the fundamentals. I was able to teach her how to round the bases, how to swing down on the ball, how to start hitting the ball consistently, all that. It was great fun.

I guess I shouldn't have been surprised. Besides the baseball heritage running through her family, we even had a history of a girl playing competitive baseball with boys. My sister Kim was on my team until I was young teenager, and she was one of the first girls anywhere to play at that level. She even appeared on the Mike Douglas TV show because of it when she was about twelve. And my older sister Dana had played competitively too, then switched to softball and field hockey.

For Christina, baseball was just another area of interest she excelled in. It seemed to me she was eager to try just about anything. She wanted to sing in the church choir because she saw other kids doing it. Plus she told her mom she wanted to be the next Christina Aguilera or Beyoncé, and she thought singing in church was a good place to start. That cracked me up. She thought she was destined to be a star at something, and that wouldn't have surprised me a bit.

⟶

Once school had started that fall of 2009 and Dallas and Christina-Taylor had their tenth and eighth birthdays, all they could talk about was our scheduled trip back east at the end of October. It appeared that the Philadelphia Phillies had a chance to make it to the World Series, and if they did, we were going to get to see some of it.

As the time drew near, the Phillies got past the Colorado Rockies and the Los Angeles Dodgers to win the National League, while the New York Yankees beat the Minnesota Twins and the Los Angeles Angels of Anaheim to win the American League. We watched the teams on TV as they split the first two games on October 28 and 29, and we planned to leave late the next day, Friday, October 30, so we could see the live game on Saturday, Halloween night.

I was working that Friday when John called and said, "Roxanna, your brother Greg called and says your mom is in the hospital."

"The hospital?"

"He says it's really, really bad."

Really, really bad? How bad could it be, whatever it was? My mother had been having some health issues, but nothing more serious than a blood clot that had been easily treated. She was fit, she ate well, did not drink or smoke, and she looked a lot younger than her seventy-four years.

Maybe I was in denial, but I just couldn't imagine something that serious could crop up so quickly. This was a woman who watched *Dr. Oz* every day, kept up on nutrition, and read everything she could about all the latest health trends. She took good care of herself, and I always told myself that she would live to be ninety and see Dallas and Christina-Taylor graduate from high school and college, marry, and have kids of their own.

I said, "John, I'm really busy here. Can you find out any more details and call me back later if—"

"I think you need to go to the hospital."

"Well, see what you can find out and call me back."

John called me back right away and said, "You need to go. I don't know any details, but apparently she called 9-1-1 herself and was taken to Northwest Hospital, but then they airlifted her to St. Joseph's."

St. Joseph's? That place—a really nice, modern facility on the other side of town—specialized in neurology. I headed there immediately, praying as I went, "Lord, let this be something minor."

As soon as I saw my mother in the emergency room, I knew she would not recover. She was hooked to a monitor and was apparently technically still alive, but—there's no other way to say it—she looked dead. My brother Greg and my uncle Red, Mom's brother-in-law, were sobbing.

We went upstairs to the Intensive Care Unit, where we met with the neurosurgeon. He told us she had suffered a brain aneurysm and showed us her brain scan. He shook his head. "I'm supposed to tell you that we could operate, but if it were my mother, I wouldn't put her through that. It wouldn't be successful anyway."

Hard as that was to hear, I sensed the doctor's compassion and could tell he was a man of faith. I think he knew that we knew where Mom would go when she died, so we didn't have that desperation to keep her alive at all costs. We would grieve, but we also knew we could rest in what the Bible calls "that blessed hope" that we would see her again.

Regardless, I was reeling. There had been no time to prepare for this or to get my mind around it, no time even for a good-bye.

Before we did anything final, I knew Greg and I needed to get our brother Paul on the phone in northern California and get his blessing. We certainly couldn't pull the plug—because, in essence, that was what we were going to have to do—or donate her organs without his input. And at this point, he knew nothing.

Of all days for him not to be at work or be carrying his cell phone. He was at the dentist for a long time and was out of touch, making it a long, long day. Meanwhile John called and wanted to know if I wanted him to come. I told him it was more important to collect the kids off the bus.

"I could bring them," he said.

"No, I don't want them to see her like this. It'll probably be a while before I get home, so you need to tell them."

When I finally reached Paul, he was, of course, as stunned as I had been. By then I had heard all the details from emergency medical personnel and the police, so I was able to tell him what happened.

"She called 9-1-1 and told them she had a horrible headache. Typical Mom, she told them, 'I won't be able to answer the door, but don't break it down. There's a kitchen window my daughter can get through, so you can get through there if you're under 5'9". I'm in the family room.'"

I told Paul that they had transported her to the nearest hospital, then airlifted her to St. Joseph's. Paul gave his permission for me to do whatever I needed to do and said he would be on the next plane out—which would arrive well after midnight.

It had all happened so suddenly that I had to fight to hold myself together. There was so much to do, so many things to think about. I wanted to be with her as long as I could, and I also wanted to ensure that her every wish was honored. I had never expected such decisions to have to be made so early, but two things she had been clear about: when her time came, she wanted her organs donated, and she wanted to be cremated.

When life support was removed and she was on a morphine drip to guarantee she would not suffer, I sat with her for about an hour before she passed peacefully. I was so grateful for that. I made sure her organs were donated and all the paperwork done, then finally trudged to my car.

For so long she had been both parents to me and both grand-parents to my kids. We'd been back in Arizona just over two years, and yet it seemed we had just gotten there and that Dallas and Christina-Taylor were finally really getting to know her.

Driving home alone after the sudden, wrenching loss of a loved one is something I don't wish on anyone and something I never wanted to do again. I know I was in emotional shock, and eager as I was to get back to John and the kids and the security of our home, I was numb.

When I arrived home at about 8:30 that evening, John gathered me in his arms and held me. I asked through my tears if he had told the kids, and he nodded. They were supposed to be in bed, but soon they came padding out and hugged me. I could tell Dallas was still confused and a little removed from the reality of it, but Christina-Taylor was crying.

She was full of questions, so I stayed up with her for a while, just talking. I knew the next few days would be hard. Our trip back east was off, of course, and I would need John to handle taking the kids trick or treating the next evening in a younger neighborhood, as I would not be up to that. But it was important to me to let Christina talk that night and to tell her as much as I could. It was a Friday, so there was no school the next day anyway.

"Is Grandma in heaven now?" she said.

"Yes."

"Why did she have to go so soon? She wasn't even sick."

"It was just time," I told her. "She had a really bad headache, but she did not suffer long."

Christina-Taylor nodded. And then, as was so typical of her, though she was sad for herself, she was thinking of me. She said, "I'm sorry you lost your mom. She should not have had to go to heaven so soon."

I couldn't argue with that.

I explained cremation and said that before that was done, they would take some of Grandma's organs and use them for others who needed them. "That was what she wanted, because, as you know, she was always very giving and wanting to help people."

Christina-Taylor was wide-eyed. "I want to do that too," she said.

"Oh, you have a lifetime before you need to think about that. But when you're old enough to drive, you can have that put on your driver's license, so whenever anything happens to you after that, you can donate your organs."

⟡

In the middle of November we held my mother's memorial service as a come-and-go-as-you-please open house at Tohono Chul restaurant, which is set in a beautiful nature park. Photos of her were displayed in a private room with her ashes, and many of her friends—and of course her whole family—came to pay their respects. Greg sang and Paul spoke, and even Dallas and Christina-Taylor tearfully talked of their grandma.

The next day we scattered some of her ashes at the home she had lived in for so many years. This made Christina-Taylor very sad, and she whispered to me that she would like a small box of her grandmother's ashes to keep in her room. They're still there.

⟡

I had never before experienced what so many people talk about—forgetting your loved one is gone when things come up that you want to ask or tell them. More than once I had a question only Mom could answer, and I'd reach for the phone, only to be stabbed anew by the painful reality of her death.

My brothers and I decided to keep her house and rent it out rather than sell it, because of the sluggish real estate market. It fell to me to clean out the whole place. Talk about pain. The kids helped too, but how melancholy it was to discover nearly seventy-five years' worth of memorabilia. She had saved every single card Dallas and Christina-Taylor had ever sent her, many of them hand-made. She even had cards my brothers and I had made for her when we were kids.

I took my time with that project, doing it in small blocks of time over several months, from after her memorial into the beginning of 2010. After work each day, I would spend a few hours going through everything.

A stark reminder of how she left us came when I discovered a spot of blood on the floor of the family room. I don't know whether the aneurysm caused her to bleed from her mouth or nose, or if perhaps she suffered a wound when she fell.

My mother had just bought Christina-Taylor a bunch of new clothes for her birthday and the new school year, and frequently she would come out of her room with a new outfit, announcing, "Grandma bought me this."

I could tell from her look that she deeply missed my mother. One of the very special dresses my mother insisted on paying for was the one I found for Christina-Taylor's First Communion, scheduled for the following May. I wanted it to be just right and was able to select one that was beautiful without being ostentatious. My mother loved it and was looking forward, as the family matriarch, to hosting the festivities the next spring. I told her she didn't have to pay for the dress too, but she wouldn't have it any other way.

How sad that Christina-Taylor's grandma would not be there for her First Communion. But she was a strong little girl, and she knew my mother would want her to just keep marching on with her life.

Leaving the Super Walmart at about 7:27 a.m., Saturday, January 8, 2011, the shooter drives the family Chevy Nova through a red light at Cortaro Road and Interstate 10 and is stopped by an officer of the Arizona Game and Fish Department.

CHAPTER EIGHT

PRELUDE TO DISASTER

FEAR NOT, FOR I AM WITH YOU;
BE NOT DISMAYED, FOR I AM YOUR GOD.
I WILL STRENGTHEN YOU, YES, I WILL HELP YOU,
I WILL UPHOLD YOU WITH MY RIGHTEOUS
RIGHT HAND (ISAIAH 41:10).

Life was different for Christina-Taylor without Grandma. Oh, she still had fun. We all did. But we missed everything my mother had brought to our family.

During the 2009 holidays, Christina-Taylor got to do again what she so loved—sing with my friend Katy Martin and her husband, Doug. They are professional singers and old friends of ours; in fact, Katy sang a duet with my brother Greg at our wedding.

Then she caught the bouquet and Doug caught the garter, and they eventually married.

Doug had played trumpet for Ray Charles, and his and Katy's band, Katy & Company, performs in Arizona and California at high-end weddings and fancy corporate parties.

For more than ten years they played several hours nightly during the week, with Doug at the keyboard and Katy singing, at the Loews Ventana Canyon Resort in Tucson. We loved to go hear them at least once a month, but especially during the holidays. Occasionally Katy would invite Christina-Taylor on stage to either just stand with her or dance with her, but also to sing with her— because the patrons loved it.

Katy happened to lose her grandmother the same month my mother died, so she and Christina-Taylor had that in common. Katy wrote me:

> Christina would be on the edge of her chair, just chomping at the bit to come up and sing with me. Sometimes she would pull on the microphone so she could sing along.
>
> She always stood with good posture and poise, as if she belonged on stage. At Christmas during the annual tree lighting ceremony at the Loews resort, I let her sing the echoes all by herself on "Do You Hear What I Hear?" and she was a real pro! We dedicated the song to our grandmothers. Christina sparkled and was always a star.

If anything, Dallas and Christina-Taylor grew closer. The time she might have spent with just her grandmother she now spent with him. They had been very close for many years, but now there was no question that they depended on each other as more than siblings. They were also best friends.

Christina-Taylor also took over the charity torch from her grandmother. Now she had even more reason to get deeply involved in humanitarian efforts, like the Kids Helping Kids charity. She and her classmates helped raise money and provide clothes and food and even books for needy children.

It was as if Christina-Taylor's life was shifting into high gear. Every time I turned around she had a new interest, a new passion. And she would throw herself wholeheartedly into each one. She had always been big and tall for her age and was an encourager, excited about life, and a natural leader. It was obvious she was going places, but would she ever limit herself to one thing long enough to make it a career? It was too early in her life to be concerned about that.

Her goal for January of 2010 was to do gymnastics, something she hadn't done since she was a small child in Pennsylvania. I knew better than to try to talk her out of anything. She already excelled at the dance academy in ballet, hip-hop, and jazz, amazing for a big-boned eight-year-old who was already the tallest kid in her class and whose parents were 6'4" and almost 5'9". All I said was, "Are you sure you want to be a gymnast?"

She said, "Oh, yeah!" and that was that. Of course, she proved good at gymnastics too. Her personality shone through and her performances reminded me of the difference between her and other girls her age who were scared to be in the spotlight. Christina-Taylor lived for it. At one dance recital, she didn't simply endure her routine and run for the shadows like many did, but she departed from the routine at the end and blew the audience a kiss!

I had always thought she was unique, of course, but even her goals—as general and scattershot as they might be—veterinarian, senator, president, singer, dancer, star—seemed different from the typical goals of kids her age.

Encouraging to me was that for all her gifts and talents and dreams, it wasn't all about her. Christina-Taylor often talked about others, especially people who needed help. Even her determination to get good grades was less about excelling for her own sake than to qualify for a college she could graduate from and make a real difference in the world.

It happened that in May of 2010, Christina-Taylor's gymnastics recital fell on the same weekend as her First Communion. That was a big deal for her, because while her extended family might not have come for just the gymnastics, they showed up for the First Communion and got to see her at both events.

John's parents came from the East Coast, my brother Paul and his wife, Anne Marie, came from northern California, Aunt Kim was there from northern California, and of course my local brother, Greg, was there. Paul is Christina-Taylor's godfather, and my best friend, Heather Grant (also of northern California) is her godmother. It was great to have her there too. Suzi and Bill Hileman came and joined us for the luncheon.

Christina-Taylor's First Communion ceremony was remarkable because she was one of only two involved that day, so they got plenty of attention. When I went through it years before, I was just one in a long line of kids.

Afterward we hosted about a hundred friends and family in the Gold Room, a fancy restaurant at the Westward Look Resort about five minutes from our church. I had told Christina-Taylor that this would be a very expensive party in her honor and so she had to earn it with good grades. Of course, there was really no way we *weren't* going to have it, and she strived for straight A's all the time anyway.

⌒

Naturally I had no way of knowing that the summer of 2010 would be our last with Christina-Taylor, but for some reason we crammed it full of travel and activity. We went on the road with John, starting in the La Jolla/San Diego area of California, up to Los Angeles, then all the way out to Cape Cod, to Philadelphia to watch the Phillies, down to North Carolina, and Florida—including Animal Kingdom, getting to see Blue Man Group, and many other unforgettable experiences.

By the time Christina-Taylor started playing fall Little League in 2010, she had become one of the best hitters on her team. And her relationship with John grew even deeper. She loved to learn and talk strategy, something he looks for in big-league prospects. Not enough young kids want to do that, even the superstars.

Again, I had not tried to talk her out of baseball, but I did suggest that she might prefer to play soccer with her girlfriends. "You're pretty good at it, and even your one girl teammate last year is playing soccer instead of baseball this year." I just wanted Christina-Taylor to have fun, and I wanted to be sure she didn't feel she had to play baseball because of her dad and grandfather.

"Maybe you play soccer now, do dance and gymnastics after that, then play softball in the spring?"

"No," she said. "I don't want to just do what everybody else does. I want to play baseball. I'm a good player."

> *John: One day during the season she came to me and said, "Dad, the boys say girls shouldn't really play because they can't get scholarships to play in college anyway. Is it true? Girls can't play college baseball?"*
>
> *"There haven't been many yet," I told her. I knew of a few in smaller, non-scholarship programs, but I didn't want to discourage her. "It's not that they're not allowed. If one is good enough, she could make it."*
>
> *She sat quiet for a moment. Finally she said, "I'm going to get a baseball scholarship someday. And I'm going to be the first girl in the big leagues too."*
>
> *I wouldn't have put it past her. It wasn't long before the boys were glad to have her on the team. She was one of the best players in the league. In fact, by the end of the season she was planning to play spring Little League too, which is a step up.*

One day she was under the weather and I knew she wasn't up to playing. John called the head coach and let him know she would not be coming. But when it was time for John to leave for the game, Christina-Taylor was in uniform and jumped in the car. "The team needs me," she said. Her coach still talks about that. She was a gamer.

Christina-Taylor's third grade teacher, Kathie DeKnikker, told me:

The first day Christina walked into my classroom, I got a glimpse of what was to come. The first assignment I gave the kids was to draw a picture of themselves. Christina's looked just like her, even to her T-shirt with "Girls Rock" on it and her hat jauntily tipped to one side. It showed her great personality and also her attention to detail. I would see those qualities every day that I was lucky enough to be her teacher.

Christina had a wonderful sense of humor and many times cracked us up with a witty comment. I will always remember that about her.

I could always count on Christina to add something interesting and enriching to group discussions. She had specific opinions on a variety of topics, and she didn't care who agreed. She was an independent thinker.

One day the kids shared what they would like to be as adults. Many had a vague idea of one thing they might like to be, but Christina had a list ranging from dancer to geologist to professional baseball player. No one scoffed. Her classmates had seen her in action and knew she would accomplish anything she set her mind to.

Christina's kindness and gentleness were apparent too, especially whenever she talked of Dallas. It was obvious they had a very special relationship.

That picture of Christina is in my box of treasures I have collected over a long career. I find myself smiling when I think about her beautiful smile and engaging personality. She will always be in my heart.

One thing I wanted Christina-Taylor involved in and thought she would enjoy—because of her interest in politics—was student council. I had been a member when I was a kid, and—assuming you couldn't run for it until you were in fourth grade—I had planned to recommend it to Christina-Taylor the next school year. I was surprised when she came home from third grade that fall and said she wanted to run for student council.

And did she have plans! After seeing the local and national campaigns her grandmother had been involved in, Christina wanted lots of posters and brochures. John and I laughed and reminded her it was elementary school, not a national campaign.

I could tell my mother had gotten to her during the campaigns when Christina-Taylor said, "I want to be like strong, powerful women leaders, like Hillary Clinton and Nancy Pelosi and Gabrielle Giffords."

John: The problem was that as eager as Christina-Taylor was to do this—and of course she wanted to run on a platform of "hope and change" and assure her classmates that they could come to her with anything—she told me that the race had really begun about a month before. She was afraid she would be hopelessly behind opponents who had already rallied their friends to their causes.

I told her, "What's important is your message. What one thing do you want your class to know about you?"

She said, "That I'll speak for them and fight for what they want and not what I want."

"That's a great message. Write that out, from your heart, and we'll put it in a one-page flyer you can pass out at school."

"But everybody else is way ahead."

Even though I'm a Republican, I knew she was an Obama fan, and I couldn't deny he had done something right. I said, "Just do what the president did. Talk about what people want and need. Put the emphasis on them."

She got on the computer and made a big poster/brochure with a picture of her from our visit to Cape Cod. It read:

Vote for Christina for Student Council

I would like your vote today so I can help you get what you want out of our school. I will work hard to make Mesa Verde a better place for all of us. Do you have good ideas to help our school? Then vote for Christina-Taylor Green and I will make it happen!

I helped her run off a bunch of them, and she wanted more. I finally had to tell her she had enough.

Three days later she won the election and joined the student council.

⌒

Christina-Taylor's birthday was always a challenge, because as happy a day as it was for her, it was one of melancholy and sorrow for the country. September 11, 2010, was her ninth, and while by now she understood the grim significance of the national anniversary, she still wanted me to bake a cake of her favorite colors—pink and purple—and put red, white, and blue flags on it. My mother had been a great cook and often made Christina's favorites on holidays and birthdays, so I felt the pressure of trying to reach a high standard. We all really missed Grandma on special days.

One of the highlights of 2010 for our family came during the fall school break Arizona has every October. Some years we decided to just stay home, and the year before we hadn't felt like traveling because my mother had just passed away. This time we decided it was time to make the break extraordinary.

We traveled to northern California to visit my brother and his wife and my best friend, Heather Grant, so Christina-Taylor could see both her godparents. John's sister Kim also lived out that way, so it became a great family time. We spent a week, getting a few days with everybody, going to the Monterey Aquarium, and to the beach in Marin where John taught the kids to body surf in wet suits. We also visited San Francisco and enjoyed Chinese food, saw the Golden Gate Bridge, and Christina-Taylor got to ride horses. It was just the best vacation.

A month later John and I organized a fundraiser for his old friend and baseball colleague P. J. Carey and his wife, Katherine. P. J. had worked for the Phillies years before, and we reconnected with them when they moved to Arizona. He's now senior adviser for player development with the Dodgers, so John enjoys getting to work with him.

Both P. J. and Katherine contracted cancer, so we staged a game for them at a Scottsdale stadium and auctioned off baseball memorabilia. Amazingly, Christina-Taylor's experience with my mother in fundraising events really came to the fore and she was a big help. I was impressed that she seemed willing to do anything for the cause, even helping load the van with boxes of bats and balls and other collectible items.

⌁

Christmas of 2010 was at first pressure-filled for me, because again I had to take over the cooking and baking slack from my mother. The kids had been used to all kinds of goodies from her, and I had been spoiled over the years by her producing her specialties. One thing Christina-Taylor kept asking about was one of my mother's favorites: authentic Mexican tamales.

She had watched Grandma make these every year, but what Christina-Taylor really wanted was to make them herself with me and with her best friend, Serenity Hammerich, and her mother, Sonia. Sonia and I had become close because of the friendship between the girls. The Hammerichs are Hispanic too, so this became an outstanding occasion for all of us.

We met at the Hammerich home during the second week of December and had a wonderful time making a huge batch of tamales and splitting them up so Christina-Taylor and I could take ours home and they could keep theirs. We talked about that time and enjoyed those tamales for days.

⌁

We had one more big trip planned, and I held it out like a carrot to the kids, again telling them they had to earn it. The plan was that if they kept their grades up, we would have our own Christmas at home a few days ahead of the actual holiday, then we would fly to the Caribbean and spend Christmas and New Year's with Nana and

Pop Green. They had a home in the Turks and Caicos Islands, and for the first time I had invited both my brothers. They had never been there before. Unfortunately, Greg had to stay home and keep an eye on Uncle Red and Aunt Elida, but Paul and Anne Marie were able to join us.

Even though I knew we were leaving for the Caribbean the next day, I made sure to fully decorate our house for Christmas, tree and all. Our own Christmas with just the four of us was special, and Christina-Taylor finally got the guitar she had been asking for. Again I was struck that my mother's musical bent was being passed down. My brother Greg plays the guitar too, and Christina-Taylor had even been to the recording studio with him, so I think that's where she may have caught the bug.

We hadn't been to Turks and Caicos Islands for several years, but just the memories of some of our favorite trips kept us excited during the flight. It was so great that Dallas and Christina-Taylor's aunt and uncle could come along, and we were determined to make the most of it.

Besides enjoying traditional Christmas Eve and Christmas Day celebrations there, including a big meal, we celebrated Nana's birthday on the twenty-sixth and John's and my sixteenth wedding anniversary on New Year's Eve. The kids got to go on a submarine with Uncle Paul and Aunt Anne Marie, and we spent the rest of the time going to the beach, boating, exploring, catching glowworms in the night, and eating way too much.

More than I could have imagined, it turned out to be the trip of a lifetime. When we finally got back to Tucson on Sunday, January 2, 2011, still enjoying our festively decorated house, we had no idea we were living our last week with Christina-Taylor. She would not see another Sunday.

I recall thinking that life could not have been better. I even said to her, "Our life is so perfect." Just think of what we'd done that year: her First Communion, her gymnastics recital, traveling all over both coasts with John, excelling in Little League, being elected to student council, the trip to California, making the tamales with Serenity and her mom, Christmas here, Christmas with her aunt and uncle and Nana and Pop in the Caribbean . . .

What could have been better than that? Even Christina-Taylor told me, "It's like our family is blessed."

It sure was. We'd had a long run of really happy times.

The shooter drives home and has some sort of an altercation with his father, then leaves on foot for the desert, sometime after 7:45 a.m., Saturday, January 8, 2011.

CHAPTER NINE

THE UNSPEAKABLE

HE SAID TO ME, "MY GRACE IS SUFFICIENT FOR YOU,
FOR MY STRENGTH IS MADE PERFECT IN WEAKNESS."
THEREFORE MOST GLADLY I WILL RATHER BOAST IN MY INFIRMITIES,
THAT THE POWER OF CHRIST MAY REST UPON ME. . . .
FOR WHEN I AM WEAK, THEN I AM STRONG
(2 CORINTHIANS 12:9–10B).

I got back from the Turks and Caicos Islands refreshed and excited about 2011. The new year seemed limitless in its possibilities and opportunities.

John was still relatively new in his job as National Cross-checker for the Los Angeles Dodgers and was really enjoying the biggest professional challenge he had ever had.

Dallas was doing so well in a traditional classroom that it was easy to forget that experts had told us not so many years ago that he would likely be relegated to special schools or classes the rest of his life. Even the wonderful one-on-one aide who had been assigned him at Mesa Verde was now serving the whole class and not just him. He was in his last year before middle school and was enjoying all his activities.

Christina-Taylor remained an easy child to raise. She was happy and optimistic, eager to experience all life had to offer. I can hardly imagine her without her gleaming smile and her unflagging curiosity about anything new and exciting. She had just come off a wonderful fall baseball season and was going to jump back into gymnastics as soon as school started again.

At the end of that first week of school following Christmas break, Friday evening, January 7, 2011, Suzi Hileman called. It had been a while since we had talked, but she had an idea. "Congresswoman Gabrielle Giffords is having a 'Congress on Your Corner' event outside the Safeway tomorrow morning at ten. I was just wondering if the kids would want to go."

"Oh, I'm sure they would," I said. "I know Christina-Taylor would love to meet her."

The Casas Adobes Safeway is in the La Toscana Village Mall less than four miles from us. I drove past there all the time. Suzi said she would swing by and pick up the kids at about a quarter to ten the next day. "Then we'll have lunch together and I'll bring them home."

I told Suzi that sounded great.

When I mentioned it to Christina-Taylor, she said, "Oh, that will be fun! I really want to meet Mrs. Giffords."

But Dallas reminded me he had karate the next morning. I emailed Suzi and told her it would be only Christina-Taylor, and she wrote back that they would just make it a girls' outing then, maybe get pedicures and do lunch before coming home.

Here's the news release Congresswoman Giffords had put out, announcing the event:

> TUCSON—U.S. Rep. Gabrielle Giffords will host her first "Congress on Your Corner" of the year on Saturday, Jan. 8, at a supermarket in northwest Tucson. "Congress on Your Corner" allows residents of Arizona's 8th Congressional District to meet their congresswoman one-on-one and discuss with her any issue, concern, or problem involving the federal government. Giffords has hosted numerous "Congress on Your Corner" events since taking office in January 2007. As in the past, the congresswoman's staff will be available to assist constituents. Previous "Congress on Your Corner" events in Tucson, Oro Valley, Green Valley, Sierra Vista, and Douglas have attracted between 75 and 150 people.
>
> WHAT: "Congress on Your Corner" with U.S. Rep. Gabrielle Giffords WHEN: 10-11:30 a.m., Saturday, January 8, 2011 WHERE: Safeway, 7110 N. Oracle Road (southeast corner of Oracle and Ina)

That Friday evening, Christina-Taylor rode along as I dropped Dallas off about five minutes away at his best friend Spencer Garrett's house for a birthday party and sleepover.

Spencer's sister Shea and Christina-Taylor had once been best friends too, and they would always be friends, but they weren't as close anymore. Yet as soon as we got back home, the phone rang. It was Spencer and Shea's mother, Heidi. She and I knew each other well, as she was a former teacher and well connected at the school, and we worked closely together in the PTO. "Right after you left," she said, "Shea said she wished Christina could come back and spend a little time with her, maybe have some birthday cake and be here when Spencer opens his presents."

Christina-Taylor, ever our social butterfly, loved that idea. So I took her back. It would be for just a few hours, because neither Heidi nor I thought it would be a good idea to add two little girls to a boys' birthday party. Boys just don't seem to generate the drama girls do.

Just before ten I drove back to pick up Christina-Taylor and was pleased to learn she'd had a really good time. "No catfights?" I teased.

She laughed. "No! Everybody got along great and it was fun."

Later, not long after Christina-Taylor and I had gone to bed, John—a bit of a night owl—heard her cry out. He discovered she was having some sort of a bad dream, so he suggested she sleep with me and he would sleep in her bed. When he brought her to our room, I asked her what was wrong, but she just mumbled something I couldn't make out and was soon asleep again.

Christina-Taylor was not prone to nightmares, and she only occasionally slept in our bed. I'll always wonder if she was having some sort of a premonition. Looking back on it now, what a privilege it was to have my beautiful princess with me all through her last night on earth.

She was up early Saturday morning, happily chattering about going with Mrs. Hileman to meet Congresswoman Giffords. "I'm going to ask her about global warming." I had little doubt that she would. In fact, Christina Taylor would want to be right up front, as close to the congresswoman as she could get, and I doubted she would ask only one question. I smiled, thinking they'd probably have to eventually cut her off and move on to the next person.

Dallas had class at Hoffman Karate and Tae Kwon Do from nine to ten that morning, just a few minutes' drive from our home. The Hoffman family, who ran the place, put a lot of emphasis on attendance, and Dallas would never miss unless he was sick. You can imagine how grateful I am for that now. Had it not been for that class that morning, he would have been standing right next to Christina-Taylor outside the Safeway.

When I got back from dropping Dallas off, Christina was wearing her blue sapphire birthstone earrings, a pink top with a Caribbean-style tropical scene with "Wish You Were Here" on it, dark skinny jeans, and tennis shoes with lots of sparkle. She looked like a real girly girl.

At just after nine, John left in his grubby clothes to meet some contractors at a little house about three miles north of us that we had bought to fix up and rent out. My morning would be full of chores around the house as soon as Christina-Taylor was off.

Right on schedule at 9:45 a.m., Suzi Hileman pulled up in her little white car, and I followed Christina-Taylor as she bounded out and jumped into the front seat. Suzi and I traded pleasantries and I told her how much I appreciated this. "And when do you expect to be back so I can be sure to be here?"

"Well, afterward we'll get our toes done and grab a little lunch, so figure three hours?"

"Sounds good. See you then. Oh! Christina run back in and get a hoodie in case it doesn't warm up."

As she hurried back into the house, Christina-Taylor called out, "Mom, I don't really need one!"

But it was cool, even for January, and who knew whether it would really heat up the way the weatherman was predicting? She came back out carrying her hoodie that had a peace sign and "Justice and Peace" on it. As she got back into the car, Christina-Taylor rolled her eyes and said again, "I don't need it, Mom."

"Better safe than sorry," I said. "You can tie it around your waist or leave it in the car. Just have it handy."

Suzi assured me she would make sure Christina wore it if it was cold.

I made sure Christina-Taylor's seatbelt was fastened and told her I loved her.

"Love you too," she said, and they were off.

A few minutes later it was time to go get Dallas. We got home a little after ten. He went to play and I started my chores. At around 10:30, the phone rang. It was Suzi Hileman's husband.

"Hi, Bill."

"Roxanna, listen," he said, his voice tight. "I just got a call that Suzi and Christina are at the University Medical Center."

"What happened?" I said. "Were they in an accident?"

"I wasn't told anything, just that we need to get there. I'm not sure I know where that is."

"It's on Campbell just south of Speedway Boulevard. Are they in the ER, or—?"

"No idea."

"All right. Well, that's where we should start anyway. Thanks for letting me know, Bill. We'll see you there."

UMC was just over twelve miles to the southwest, and my route would take me right past where Suzi and Christina-Taylor were supposed to see Congresswoman Giffords. Had this, whatever it was, happened on the way there? I figured I'd find out soon enough.

As soon as I hung up I called John's cell and got his voice mail. I could just picture him leaving his phone on the counter in the kitchen of the rental house and wandering around with a contractor or two. "Call me as soon as you can," I said. "Bill Hileman just called and said Suzi and Christina are at UMC. Don't know if it was an accident or what, but we have to get over there right away. Hurry home so we can go."

Dallas likes his routine and doesn't always deal well with change, so I needed to get him started getting ready. "Get your shoes on and grab a jacket, because we have to go to the hospital."

"What's going on, Mom?"

"Christina and Suzi have been in some kind of an accident, I think, so as soon as Dad gets here, we're going to go."

"A car accident?"

"I'm not sure. Just pray for them that everything will be okay, all right?" That served at least to get him away from whatever he was doing and start getting ready.

We don't wear it on our sleeves, but praying is a normal thing for our family. We don't just pray when we're in trouble. We pray a lot, before meals, before bed, whenever we feel like it. Dallas and I were both praying silently, hardly knowing what to ask for, while he got ready and I stalled, waiting for John's call or for him to show up.

Minutes began to feel like forever. I wasn't allowing myself to worry that this was terribly serious, but any parent understands the feeling of learning your child has been hurt but not knowing how badly. I always see the glass half full and, of course, want everything to be okay. I kept telling myself that they were in a safe area in broad daylight, late on a Saturday morning. Maybe somebody had pulled out in front of Suzi or something else caused a fender bender. Then, because Suzi was in her late fifties and her passenger was a nine-year-old, they were taken in for observation just to be safe.

Still, a few minutes later I called John again as Dallas and I left the house. "We're getting into the car," I told him. "We can't wait any longer. Just meet us in the ER at UMC."

I was careful to watch my speed and reminded Dallas that we both needed to keep praying. As I neared the Safeway in La Toscana Village Mall across the street from the Casas Adobes Shopping Center, I saw emergency vehicles, flashing lights, and barricades. I was going to have to take advantage of my knowledge of the area and go the back way. I took an immediate right to avoid everything and get around the shopping center.

I wound up on the south end of the strip mall and saw people wandering about and yellow police tape around the plaza. I didn't say anything to Dallas, but I now worried that if Suzi's little car got caught in a major pileup, maybe it was a more serious accident than I thought. Perhaps a truck was involved, several vehicles?

Christina-Taylor and Suzi had to be okay though, right? That's not my life; serious things don't happen to my family and friends. But it sure looked like it could have been a bad accident. I couldn't tell if Dallas was starting to put things together or not. I was concentrating on getting to UMC as quickly as possible without speeding, all the while sneaking peeks at my cell phone to see if I had missed a call from John.

"Still praying for her," Dallas said.

"Good."

I was getting nervous, but I didn't want him to see that.

By now it was 10:45 a.m., and fortunately there was little traffic on a Saturday. I reached the hospital at just before eleven, but when I followed the signs to the emergency room I found the entrance blocked off with police cars and ringed with camera crews and news trucks.

Suddenly I had a one-track mind. I needed to find a place to park so I could get in there and make sure Christina-Taylor was all right.

Taxi company records show a driver picks up the shooter from the Circle K at 3712 W. Cortaro Farms Road at 9:41 a.m., Saturday, January 8, 2011, and takes him to a Safeway grocery store at 7100 N. Oracle Road, north of Tucson in Pima County. At 9:54 a.m., the driver and his passenger go into the Safeway to get change.

CHAPTER TEN

THE NEWS

TRUST IN THE LORD WITH ALL YOUR HEART,
AND LEAN NOT ON YOUR OWN UNDERSTANDING;
IN ALL YOUR WAYS ACKNOWLEDGE HIM,
AND HE SHALL DIRECT YOUR PATHS (PROVERBS 3:5–6).

I finally found a spot for the car in a parking lot far from the main entrance, and Dallas and I hurried in. All I could think of was that all that commotion at the ER entrance was just another red flag. I told myself that everything would be all right once I reached Christina-Taylor. I'd had to make tough medical decisions fourteen months before for my own mother; surely I could do it again, because there was no way this could be as dire as that had been.

I just wanted answers, to know my daughter was okay. I could deal with anything else, no matter how serious.

The University of Arizona's Medical Center is a huge complex, and the main entrance is nowhere near the emergency room. I rushed up to the reception desk. "I'm Roxanna Green and my nine-year-old daughter Christina-Taylor was brought here with Mrs. Susan Hileman. Can you tell me where I can find her?"

The woman asked me to spell the names, then said, "I don't see either in the system yet, so if they're here, they're probably in the ER. Do you know how to get there from here?"

"I'll find it," I said, not wanting to waste any more time and figuring I could follow the signs. All along the way I asked people if we were heading in the right direction.

Finally I came upon a uniformed Tucson police officer, in his early thirties with close-cropped blondish brown hair. I quickly ran down the details, that I had been instructed to come here, my daughter's and Suzi's names, and asked if he knew anything about it. He was very kind and helpful and pointed, instructing me to "go right through those double doors, ma'am, and you'll be in the emergency room."

I didn't think about it at the time, but as I reflect on it I realize he probably knew a lot more than he let on. What had happened would have been a big deal for the Tucson police.

In the ER I found a few dozen people milling around and looking tense, like they too were waiting for answers. I spotted Bill Hileman, who looked panicky.

"They're telling me Suzi's not here!" he said. "But if Christina is, Suzi has to be, right?"

"Of course. Maybe they're just not in the system yet, Bill. Does anybody know what happened?"

"Nobody's told me anything," he said, "except that my wife's not here. You ask them. See what they tell you."

I went to a woman behind the counter and introduced myself, asking about Christina-Taylor Green. She said, "Wait here just a minute." Another red flag. I was a nurse, not to mention a mother who had been to the ER before. That was not a typical response. I could tell by the way she looked at me that she knew exactly who Christina-Taylor was and what had happened to my daughter.

Now I was convinced that Christina had been in an accident and that she had been seriously injured. Otherwise, the woman would have just told me what happened to her, where she was being treated, and not to worry. That was not the message I was getting.

When the woman returned, she said, "Follow me to the elevator. I need to take you upstairs." Though she was trying to be pleasant and efficient, I suspected her look and her tone. I knew she knew more than she was letting on, but I couldn't get a thing out of her. She looked as if she would rather be anywhere but right there right then.

I signaled to Bill Hileman, who hurried over. "I think they're taking me to see Christina-Taylor right now. If I find out anything about Suzi, I'll let you know."

As the elevator rose to the sixth floor, the woman asked if Dallas or I wanted anything to drink. I felt for her because she was trying to be so helpful, but something to drink was the last thing on my mind. "What I want," I said, "is for you to tell me what has happened and what is going on with Christina-Taylor."

"I'm sorry, I can't," she said, "but someone is going to come and talk to you."

I didn't know if she couldn't tell me because she didn't know or because she wasn't allowed to. It was then I realized that she was in regular business clothes and was not an ER nurse. She had to be some kind of a social worker or administrator, another red flag.

I didn't like where this was headed, but I did not even allow myself to think the worst. Whatever it was, I believed I could handle it. And knowing Christina-Taylor's character and personality, I knew she could too.

I was hoping for the best and working to stay calm, if for no other reason than Dallas's sake. The woman led us into a small room with a table and a few chairs. It was not a typical waiting room, but I had the feeling we might be there a while.

"Dallas," I said, "would you like her to get you some water?"

He nodded, and the woman seemed relieved to have something to do. She got us each a bottle of water, and I sat down, more convinced than ever that whatever this was, it was worse than I had originally thought. I envisioned a car-truck crash, some debilitating injuries, maybe a long therapy and recovery time. Regardless, we would handle it; that was the kind of family we were.

I asked the woman if there was a restroom nearby, and she showed me where it was. I asked Dallas if he wanted to go with me. He shook his head, and she said she would stay with him.

As I entered the small bathroom I imagined that Christina-Taylor was in emergency surgery. That had to be why no one could tell me anything yet; they didn't know anything.

Before I left to return to the other room, I realized this was probably going to be the last time I would get to be alone before someone came to talk to us. I was desperate and glad Dallas didn't have to see me that way. I knelt on the floor and folded my hands. "Lord," I said, "please take care of Christina-Taylor. But if it's really, really bad, just let her go and don't let her suffer. Take her; don't let her be in pain."

For once I was grateful for Dallas's autism. Another eleven-year-old might have been suspicious of all this and started putting two and two together. But he tended to focus on the moment. He had his water, he was waiting for me, and whatever else was going on was not relevant to him just then.

When I returned, the woman and Dallas had been joined by a couple of other people wearing name badges and civilian clothes. I could tell they were there to tend to us, but I still wasn't putting it all together. They introduced themselves, and one of them began interacting with Dallas. Still, no one would tell me anything.

I was glad to see a Bible on a small table. I grabbed it and held it in my lap, and then I called John one more time, finally getting through.

"I'm on my way, Roxanna," he said, "but what is going on? Is Christina all right?"

"I don't know, but hurry, please. The ER entrance is blocked off, so park out front." I told him we were on the sixth floor and what room he should come to. Thank God he's a calm and positive person. "Okay," he said, "I'm about halfway there. See you soon."

As soon as I got off the phone a doctor in surgical scrubs came in, followed by a police officer and three nurses with "ICU" on their badges. The nurses' eyes were full of tears and they awkwardly lined up on one wall while the doctor sat across the table from me. To me he looked miserable, and I knew this had to be bad. Just like when I was watching the 9/11 attacks on TV the day Christina was born, I pinched myself to be sure it wasn't a nightmare.

The woman who had brought us to the room asked, "Ma'am, do you want to wait for your husband? How close is he?"

"No," I said, "I can't wait any longer. I need to know right now."

For all I knew, John would hit traffic, and if Christina-Taylor had serious injuries, I wanted to see her as soon as possible and make any decisions necessary as to her care. If there was any way I could help move this thing along, that's what I wanted to do.

With that the surgeon broke down and could barely speak. "I'm so sorry," he managed. "We worked and worked and we tried our best, but we just couldn't save her."

Couldn't save her? She's gone?

"She died of a bullet wound through her chest from the back. There was a shooting at the political meeting, and Congresswoman Giffords was killed too."

The nurses standing behind him were weeping openly now. The surgeon leaned across the table and we held each other. "We tried everything," he said, sobbing.

"I know," I said. "I know you did. Thank you so much. Thanks to all of you."

I was desperately trying to compose myself for Dallas. He rose and came to me. "Are we gonna see Christina now?" he said.

I couldn't believe he could have heard all that I heard and still ask that, but I didn't want to hurt his feelings. Yet he had to know. I said, "No, honey, she passed away and she's in heaven with God now."

He stared at me and I could see the truth wash over him. We both broke down and just sat holding each other and crying.

Just then John walked in, and as I rose to go to him, I could see on his face that he didn't want to hear what he feared had happened. The surgeon immediately told him what he had told me. John's eyes narrowed and his face and neck reddened. "Do they know who did this?" he said, teeth clenched.

"Yes."

"And did they get him?"

"They got him."

"Good."

John and Dallas and I held each other and wept. Finally I pulled away and asked the doctor, "Would she have suffered?" The last thing I wanted was for Christina-Taylor to have endured an even more horrible end.

"No, ma'am," he said, still overcome. "That I'm sure of. It appears she may have had time to spin away from the sound of the gunfire, but the bullet she took hit both her heart and lungs. She would have felt the impact, but it's likely she felt no pain and was gone before she hit the ground. We did everything we could to bring her back. I'm so sorry."

In a strange way, while still trying to get my head around all this, I was grateful to hear that from an expert. If this could have been worse, it would be because I imagined her in agony and crying out for me. I would not have been able to live with that.

Finally the doctor collected himself. He said, "Would you like to see her? I believe they've fixed her up and she's presentable."

I wondered if that would be okay for Dallas, but there was no question in his mind. He definitely wanted to see her. On the way down the hall the nurses asked whether it would be all right if they joined us. I assured them it was. Someone asked if we wanted a priest, and I assured them we did.

At 9:58 a.m., Saturday, January 8, 2011, United States Representative Gabrielle Giffords' office tweets from an iPad: "My 1st Congress on Your Corner starts now. Please stop by to let me know what is on your mind or tweet me later."

CHAPTER ELEVEN

THE SANCTUARY

BE ANXIOUS FOR NOTHING, BUT IN EVERYTHING
BY PRAYER AND SUPPLICATION,
WITH THANKSGIVING, LET YOUR REQUESTS BE
MADE KNOWN TO GOD (PHILIPPIANS 4:6).

Later we would find out that Mrs. Giffords had not been killed, but seriously wounded instead. We would also learn that nineteen people had been shot and that six died. Original reports said five had died on the scene and Christina-Taylor at the hospital—but that proved to be a technicality. The fact was that she was not pronounced dead until medical personnel had exhausted all efforts.

I appreciate that no one wanted to give up on her and that she was attended to on the ground, in the ambulance, and in the ER.

I imagine many of those working on her were parents, saw a precious child with her whole life ahead of her, and tried everything they knew to bring her back. Clearly her injuries likely ended her life before she had even an inkling of what was going on. And in a strange way, that was some small comfort in the midst of horror.

It also wasn't long before I realized that we had been directed from the ER not to a traditional waiting room but rather to a family room where people were informed of their losses. It suddenly made sense, too, why the woman behind the desk in the ER was not a nurse but a social worker, and those people who joined us in the family room were actually government agency personnel, homicide survivor counselors. Hard as it had to be for them, they were experienced and compassionate, and they were wonderful with all of us.

I don't have to tell you this was the worst day of my life, and it won't surprise you to know that I pinched myself several more times, praying it was a terrible dream. I don't know where I got the strength to even walk down the hall to see her one last time, to interact with the nurses, to answer questions. All I knew was that I wanted to be with her, to say good-bye in my own way.

The wife and mother in me was thinking of John and Dallas at the same time. The feeling of having part of my very flesh ripped from me in an instant somehow told me how devastating this had to be for Christina-Taylor's father and brother. How they loved her!

John is a big man, a man's man, a former athlete. Christina-Taylor was his princess, his little sweetheart, and he adored her with everything that was in him.

Dallas had grown so close to his little sister that people who saw them together were amazed. They rarely squabbled and were always quick to hug and look out for each other. We traveled so much as a family that they had to become best friends. They laughed easily and kidded each other and truly enjoyed each other's company.

As we neared the room where we would find Christina-Taylor, I still didn't know if I was doing the right thing by allowing Dallas to see her body. The death of a loved one is traumatic for anyone, but to a boy of eleven who also has Asperger's Syndrome? I recall how impressionable I was at that age. Some will say it was necessary for closure. Others will say it could have scarred him. All I can say is that he really wanted to see her, and at the time it seemed the right thing to do.

We're carefully monitoring him, naturally, but so far since then he has seemed remarkably well-adjusted to his loss. He grieves, he mourns, and yet he doesn't bury his thoughts and feelings. He talks about Christina-Taylor all the time, remembering good times, fun times, trips, funny events. And when friends seem awkward and don't know what to say, he tells stories that include her and puts everyone at ease.

I know it's hard for him, and I don't want to pretend he's over it—none of us will ever be—but I have come to believe it was good for him to be able to see her that day.

It may sound strange to refer to a sterile hospital room with a dead child in the bed as a sanctuary, but there was something sacred about that place that day. The three ICU nurses stood respectfully off to the side, quietly weeping.

And there lay my beautiful angel, covered from her toes to just under her arms, her little hands folded over her tummy. She appeared to be sleeping peacefully, her long, dark hair rimming her olive face.

As John stood there, slowly shaking his head, barely able to take it in, and Dallas stared, his lips pressed together, I tiptoed to the bed. I laid my hand on Christina-Taylor's cooling face, then I kissed her and covered her hands with mine. I didn't want to see the wound. I moved down to her feet and reached under the cover to caress them.

I couldn't believe it then and still find it hard to accept that less than three hours before she had been full of life, excited, rolling her eyes at my over-protectiveness, buckling her seatbelt, and telling me, "Love you too."

Part of me felt as if I'd been run over by a truck. I don't know how I remained upright. John and Dallas and I took turns standing near her, holding each other.

A young priest in beautiful vestments knocked softly on the door. When we welcomed him in he gathered us a few feet from Christina-Taylor and said, "Bless you. I'm so sorry for your loss."

"Thank you, Father."

And then he prayed the traditional Catholic prayer for the dead: "God our Father, Your power brings us to birth, Your providence guides our lives, and by Your command we return to dust.

"Merciful Father, hear our prayer and console us. As we renew our faith in Your Son, whom You raised from the dead, strengthen our hope that our departed sister will share in His resurrection, who lives and reigns with You and the Holy Spirit, one God, forever and ever. Amen."

Then he moved to the bed and stood over Christina-Taylor with his Bible and rosary and quoted Romans 14:7–9: "For none of us lives to himself, and no one dies to himself. For if we live, we live to the Lord; and if we die, we die to the Lord. Therefore, whether we live or die, we are the Lord's. For to this end Christ died and rose and lived again, that He might be Lord of both the dead and the living."

As we embraced him and thanked him, he gave me his card and urged us to call him at any time.

After he left, one of the nurses left too, and I felt compelled to call my brother Greg. I didn't want him or anyone else in the family to hear about this first on the news. I don't know how I held it together long enough to get out the details, but I told him that Christina-Taylor had been shot and killed and that I needed him to call our aunt and uncle and my other brother.

He said, "Roxanna, slow down. Are you sure she's gone?"

"Greg, I'm standing right here in the room with her. She's passed away."

He was nearly speechless, but he was able to tell me how shocked and sorry he was and that, of course, he would make the calls.

Then I called my best friend, Heather Grant, Christina-Taylor's godmother, in northern California. I reached her voicemail and left a message with all the details, adding, "Please call me as soon as you can."

And finally I called Heidi Garrett, the woman who had hosted Dallas for the sleepover the night before and Christina-Taylor for a few hours. When I told her what happened she said, "Oh, Roxanna, no! Christina told me she was going today, and when I heard on the news what happened, I so hoped it wasn't her!"

"Can you call the principal for me and whoever else at school needs to know?"

"Of course, but, oh, I can't believe this!"

When I got off the phone, one of the nurses asked if we were prepared to discuss organ donation. I was so glad to say that because of my own mother's death during the fall of 2009, I knew Christina-Taylor's exact wishes. I was able to get those preliminaries done and was told that someone from Donor Network would handle the rest with us by phone or online from our home later.

When we finished with those details, one of the remaining nurses stepped forward and whispered, "A lot of people are going to tell you they understand what you're going through, but of course they don't. I lost a daughter to cancer last year, so at least I have some inkling . . . "

"I'm so sorry," I said.

"Listen, I wasn't even supposed to be working today, so maybe I'm here for a reason. We're not supposed to do this, but if you would like hand- and footprints of your daughter, I know how to do that."

"That would be such a treasure," I said. "Thank you so much."

While she was gone to get what she needed to make the prints, Heidi Garrett called back. "Roxanna, are you absolutely sure about this?"

I assured her it was true. It may seem strange, even insensitive for both my brother and a good friend to ask me if I was sure my own daughter had passed away. But I understood. I could hardly believe it myself, yet there I stood for almost ninety minutes next to her body with my husband and son.

Even knowing I was in shock, I couldn't hide from the truth. Christina-Taylor had been here one instant and was gone the next. It wasn't her in that hospital bed. When she was alive, for me to have seen her lie still for an hour and a half I would have had to watch her sleep, and even then she would have tossed and turned. No, this was just her earthly shell. I knew that. And still I didn't want to leave her.

After we got the hand- and footprints, the remaining two nurses asked if we would like a final few moments alone with her, and they left. One by one we approached the bed and said our goodbyes. I kissed Christina-Taylor's cold cheek a last time and told her I loved her and that I knew she was in heaven with God and Jesus and Grandma.

As I stepped back so John could have his moment, I couldn't believe this was really happening. At that point, I had no idea who had done the shooting, but I had to wonder—no matter how angry or crazy or deluded a person had to be to open fire on a bunch of people, wouldn't seeing an innocent child there give him pause? Even if his insanity told him that people were evil and out to get him, how would that include a nine-year-old girl? I couldn't make sense of it then, and I still can't now.

Hard as it was to tear myself away, I could see in John's look that he just wanted to get Dallas out of there and have us go home and be by ourselves. Even walking to the elevator as a family of three instead of four seemed strange, and it was as if I had to concentrate just to put one foot in front of the other.

When we got off the elevator on the first floor back near the ER, there was Bill Hileman at the end of the hall. I knew they had to have located Suzi or he wouldn't still be there. He was wringing his hands.

"Is everything okay with Christina?" he said.

"No, Bill," I said. "She passed away."

"Oh, my gosh! I'm so sorry!"

He embraced me, and I said, "Is Suzi okay?"

"She was shot three times," he said, "and she's in surgery right now. They think she's going to be all right."

"I hope and pray she is," I said.

"Thank you. And again, I'm so sorry."

⁓

It was as if each of us was in his own world when we exited the hospital, but suddenly we realized we had two cars in the parking lot. "Are you going to be okay to drive?" John said.

"Yes," I said. "Are you?"

He nodded but said he didn't want me to drive home alone.

"I've got to call Tina anyway," I said. "And if we all ride home together, somebody's going to have to come back for the other car eventually."

We reluctantly agreed that John would drive Dallas home. I could see John was still conflicted, but I assured him I would be all right.

The first thing I did when I got in the car was to call my friend Tina Mead-Ramirez, who I've known since fourth grade. She lives a little more than a half hour from us on the east side of Tucson, and we'd seen each other at least a couple of times a month since we had moved back. Besides wanting to tell her what happened, I needed her, in essence, to talk me home.

Here's how she recalls that phone call:

Roxanna and I have been friends a long time, and we have an unspoken commitment to emotionally support each other, no matter what. But nothing could have prepared me to help her through the worst time of her life.

The day before, my husband Paul and I had both been diagnosed with the H1N1 virus and instructed to stay home in bed for five days until we were no longer contagious.

Late Saturday morning our son, Shay, came in to check on us and said he'd just seen on his computer that Gabrielle Giffords had been shot. We turned on the television, where it was reported that the tragedy had happened on the northwest side of Tucson and that a nine-year-old girl had been one of the victims.

I thought of my own daughter, Madison, seven years old. I could not imagine losing her. It also crossed my mind that Roxanna lived on the northwest side and that her daughter, Christina, was nine.

When the phone rang about two hours later, I was so sick I debated about answering. Paul said, "It's probably Roxanna checking to see how you're feeling."

He was right. Roxanna said, "How are you doing?"

"So sick," I said, "How are you?"

Roxanna said, "I wanted to let you know, Christina died today."

I screamed, "NO! NO! NO! NO! NO! NO!"

But I had to be strong for my friend. I told myself, *Pull it together, Tina.*

"Where are you, Roxanna?"

"Driving home from the hospital."

"Who's with you?"

"I'm by myself."

I could not believe it, and I so wanted to be with her.

"Tell me what I can do," I said.

Her voice was quavering. "Please, just start letting people know and ask them to pray."

I promised I would, and soon she said she had made it home and that John had just pulled up.

I would wait until the next day to tell my daughter. I had to really process what I was going to say. I had hoped Madison and Christina-Taylor would be lifelong friends like their mothers.

I was struck that Roxanna cared enough to ask how I was doing before she even told me her unthinkable tragedy. That is so much like her, a true friend.

All our lives have been forever changed by Christina's death. My faith and prayer get me through my darkest days, and for that I am thankful, as I am for the gift of friendship I have with Roxanna. I have never stopped praying for her.

"And now abide faith, hope, love, these three; but the greatest of these is love" (1 Corinthians 13:13).

⌒⌒

I'll always be grateful to Tina for staying with me on the phone until I pulled in at home. Maybe my asking about her health first was a defense mechanism. I was fully aware and cognizant of what had happened, and distraught as I was, I was at least in the moment. I didn't need to be committed or sedated. I was hanging on as best I could.

John and I reached the house at virtually the same time, and the three of us trudged inside to a new, bizarre reality. It was as if the life of our party was gone. The house had almost always been constantly alive with activity and chatter and laughter, largely because of Christina-Taylor.

Now we tearfully went in and sat down, not knowing what to do with ourselves. Our Christmas decorations still hung about, including Christina's stocking. Everything I looked at reminded me of her, and it was just awful. All we could do was hug each other on and off and cry.

Dallas was so sweet. We knew he was suffering every bit as much as we were, but he stayed close to us and kept asking John and me if we were okay.

Meanwhile, in Washington, D.C., President Obama released a statement:

> This morning, in an unspeakable tragedy, a number of Americans were shot in Tucson, Arizona, at a constituent meeting with Congresswoman Gabrielle Giffords. And while we are continuing to receive information, we know that some have passed away, and that Representative Giffords is gravely wounded.
>
> We do not yet have all the answers. What we do know is that such a senseless and terrible act of violence has no place in a free society. I ask all Americans to join me and Michelle in keeping Representative Giffords, the victims of this tragedy, and their families in our prayers.

—

Not long after, Senator John McCain, our Arizona senator, released his own statement:

> I am horrified by the violent attack on Representative Gabrielle Giffords and many other innocent people by a wicked person who has no sense of justice or compassion. I pray for Gabby and the other victims, and for the repose of the souls of the dead and comfort for their families. I beg our loving Creator to spare the lives of those who are still alive, heal them in body and spirit, and return them to their loved ones.
>
> Whoever did this, whatever their reason, they are a disgrace to Arizona, this country, and the human race, and they deserve and will receive the contempt of all decent people and the strongest punishment of the law.

It wasn't long before the phone started ringing, and I wondered if the calls would ever stop.

At 10:10 a.m., Saturday, January 8, 2011, the shooter approaches Congresswoman Gabrielle Giffords, who has about thirty people in line and around her, and opens fire. Six people die and thirteen are injured.

CHAPTER TWELVE

HUNKERED DOWN

I CAN DO ALL THINGS THROUGH CHRIST WHO
STRENGTHENS ME (PHILIPPIANS 4:13).

Only those who have been through something like this have any idea of the otherworldly thoughts and feelings that wash over you. On the one hand, you can hardly believe it has happened; on the other, you're so deeply, painfully aware that your life will never be the same, you can barely think past the next instant.

It's as if you yourself have been mortally wounded, that no matter what anyone else says or does, nothing can change the awful truth, nothing can make things better. As well-intentioned as loved ones and friends are—and they are truly suffering with you and for you—it seems all is lost. Your very life, your reason for being, has been robbed from you in an instant. For me, had it not been for John and Dallas, I couldn't have imagined going on. For what? I wanted to be with Christina-Taylor. I knew she was in heaven, so that's where I wanted to be.

This was not, of course, depression in its classic sense, but I sure got a glimpse of what a terrible ordeal depression must be. Nothing, nothing seemed worth doing. Standing, walking, getting something, talking, answering a question, sitting—what was the point?

Something about grief, especially when it has been thrust upon you without warning or preparation—as opposed to when an elderly family member has suffered and you know the inevitable is coming—sucks every last ounce of energy from you. Suddenly the simplest tasks seem like mountains to climb.

Our trauma had begun with the phone call from Bill Hileman and was now, just hours later, ramping up speed and taking over our lives. We had not even thought about lunch, getting the terrible news on empty stomachs and fortified with just bottles of water.

But thinking of practical matters like eating seemed petty. Plus, how does one muster the strength to walk to the kitchen, to prepare even the most uncomplicated of meals? I no more wanted to do that—despite knowing that all three of us needed fuel to live on—than I wanted to climb Mount Everest.

Yet nothing was served either by our sitting in stunned silence, barely able to move. I knew we had to force ourselves to somehow stay active, to do something, anything. Silent, introspective bereavement could eat us alive. Christina-Taylor wouldn't want that. She would want us to endure, to survive, to be strong.

I couldn't imagine it, but I felt like I owed it to her to try.

We'd been home not even an hour when the doorbell rang and an old acquaintance of mine, Stephanie Grandpre, appeared at the door. She was nearly hysterical, as anyone would be, and I was touched that she had made the effort to drive from her home more than thirty-five minutes from us. She had come, she told us, in Tina's stead, because Tina and her husband had contracted the H1N1 virus.

"Tina so desperately wanted to be here for you," Stephanie said.

It was a moment with such mixed emotions. Part of me wanted to be alone with just John and Dallas, and yet here was a dear mutual friend of Tina's and mine, one I had grown even closer to over the last couple of years, someone I enjoyed being with. (She is also an artist who has since crafted ceramic butterflies for our website, dedicated to the Christina-Taylor Green Memorial Foundation.)

I expected my brother Greg soon, because he was local, and I knew my brother Paul and his wife, Anne Marie, would get to us from northern California as soon as they could.

Naturally, none of us knew what to say or do. We weren't in any position to be hospitable, paralyzed as we were with grief. And of course Stephanie didn't expect anything else of us, yet she didn't know what to say either. Just having her sit there and cry with us was a quiet blessing.

Soon Tina's mother and stepfather showed up, and she too told us how urgently Tina wished she could be there: "She told me, 'Mom, Roxanna doesn't have a mother. Can you go and be her mother?'"

I was touched that they would drive more than an hour on Tina's behalf and serve as surrogate parents to me. They stayed about an hour and a half and Stephanie another hour and a half. It was a gift to me that they did not act as if I should play the part of a typical hostess. They merely mourned with us, which was all we were capable of.

As each left, they asked if there was anything else they could do for us, but there wasn't. We didn't want or need anything but our Christina-Taylor back, so—other than that—in a weird way we were okay.

A little later, I got a call back from Christina-Taylor's godmother and my best friend, Heather Grant, from northern California.

> **Heather:** *Roxanna and I have been friends for over twenty-five years, and we are like sisters from different mothers. We have been through so many things together that it seems at times as if we have already been friends for over a lifetime. I truly believe certain people come into our lives for a purpose. Roxanna and I have served that purpose for one another over and over again. I'm not sure what I would do without her.*
>
> *The morning of Saturday, January 8, I didn't have my kids and my plans were to clean my house and get the rest of the holiday items put away.*
>
> *My cell phone was charging, so I did not hear it when Roxanna called. At around 12:30 [Pacific time] I wanted to take my dogs to the park to run, call my mom, and call Roxanna— not knowing she had called earlier.*
>
> *I thought we would just be catching up, which we had done for years, multiple times a week and occasionally for hours at a time. As I was walking to the park, I first called my mom, who also lives in Tucson. She immediately asked if I had heard about the terrible shooting there that had wounded a congresswoman and killed a nine-year-old girl, along with others. My daughter*

Hailey was eleven and my son Camden, nine, so my heart sank as a parent and former fellow Tucsonan.

As we got off the phone I just stood there stunned, imagining this terrible thing happening where I had grown up and had always considered such a safe haven. Just as I was about to call Roxanna, her brother Paul called and asked if I had spoken to her yet. "I was just about to," I said.

He said, "There's been a tragic shooting in Tucson."

"Paul, was the nine-year-old girl Christina?"

"It was."

My whole body went weak. He and I were Christina's godparents, and we both loved her so much. I was in shock and told him how sorry I was and that I had to call Roxanna.

There was no answer, so I called John. He sounded horrible and confirmed the nightmare was true. Christina-Taylor was the apple of her dad's eye, and I felt the heartbreak in his voice. He told me Roxanna would call me back.

I felt so far away. I had to get to Tucson to somehow give my best friend and her family the support they needed. My kids loved Christina and Dallas so much that they thought of them as their cousins and best friends. How was I going to tell them? What was Dallas going to do without his sister, his best friend and guiding light?

I called my ex-husband, Scott, since my kids were with him. I just needed to be with them and to hug and comfort them before delivering this most devastating news. I told him what had happened and asked him to give me an hour and I'd be over so we could tell them.

When I got there it was clear that I had been crying, and Scott was upset too, so my kids knew something was up. The three of them had been watching the whole tragedy unfold on the news. I asked the kids if they knew there had been a nine-year-old girl shot and killed, and they nodded.

"That little girl was our Christina."

They both looked at me in horror and their eyes filled with tears. Hailey came and sat on my lap as she cried and cried. Camden wiped his eyes and gave his dad a hug, then hugged me, grabbed his bat and a ball and went to the park. He and Christina always said they were going to get married one day.

I made arrangements for Hailey and Camden and me to fly to Tucson first thing in the morning. When I finally spoke with Roxanna, what had been only a few hours seemed like a lifetime.

⟋⟍

When my brother Greg arrived, I could see over his shoulder that the press was camped out in front of the house. Trucks with telescopic satellite dishes, standing microphones, reporters milling about. "They're all out there," Greg said, face puffy and eyes red. "They want to talk to you. They want a statement."

"We're not going out there, Greg," I said. "We can't. They have to understand that."

"I told them that, but they're not going to leave until they get something."

I felt so bad for Greg. I could tell how hard Christina's death had been on him. They were close. He looked exhausted, and now he was frantic to do something about the swarming press. As he moved around the house, he said, "I asked them to respect our pri-

A LIFE TOO BRIEF—
IN PICTURES

As painful as it was to relive so much of Christina-Taylor's life for the pages of this book, John and I found it excruciating to sift through hundreds of images for this photo section. Every picture of our beloved angel sent waves of emotion crashing over us. We smiled through our tears at her beautiful smile and those dazzling eyes that saw all of life eagerly, expectantly, hopefully.

Seeing her with the people she loved and who loved her so much—especially her brother and best buddy, Dallas—made us ache anew to hold her one more time.

We console ourselves with the belief that the work we have done here will keep Christina-Taylor's memory alive and that this book will be a worthy tribute to her life of hope.

John and me on our wedding day in
Tucson, New Year's Eve, 1994.

Christina-Taylor at seven months.

Christina-Taylor with me at Conowingo, Maryland, on the Fourth of July, 2004.

Christina-Taylor and Dallas with their grandmother—my mother, Yolanda Segalini—in the spring of 2006.

Christina-Taylor with her godmother, Heather Grant, in Maryland in 2006.

Christina-Taylor
on Cape Cod
during the
summer of
2007.

Dallas and Christina-Taylor
on Turks and Caicos,
British West Indies, 2007.

Dallas and Christina
with John's parents,
Dallas and Sylvia Green,
at Citizens Bank Park,
Philadelphia, 2007.

John and me with Christina-Taylor and Dallas at Citizens
Bank Park in Philadelphia, summer 2007.

John and me with Christina-Taylor and
Dallas, visiting our home where the kids
were born—Stone Lea Farm in Conowingo,
Maryland—in 2007.

Christina with her brother,
Dallas, in 2009.

Dallas and Christina-Taylor at a Hoffman Karate class in 2009.

Dallas, John, and Christina-Taylor, in Cape Cod, summer 2008.

At a Creative Arts dance recital in Tucson in 2009.

Christina-Taylor at Stone Lea Farm in Maryland in 2009.

Hiking Tucson's Pima Canyon in the winter of 2009 (left to right): Dallas, my brother Greg Segalini, Christina-Taylor, John, me, Ann Marie, and her husband, my brother Paul Segalini.

John, Christina, Dallas, and me in Washington, D.C., summer 2009.

Singing with our friend Katy Martin (her husband, Doug, at the piano) in December 2009.

Her first year with the Pirates in the fall of 2009.

Christina with her BFF,
Serenity Hammerich, in 2009.

Christina, John, me, and Dallas at
Sabino Canyon in January 2010.

©2010 by Jon Wolf

Christina (left) with Sabrina Lee and
Father Richard Troutman at her First
Communion in the spring of 2010.

My favorite shot of the two of us, taken in Sabino Canyon (Tucson) in January 2010— the photo my brother showed to the media, January 8, 2011.

©2010 by Jon Wolf

Christina-Taylor was so proud to be elected by her classmates in the fall of 2010.

Vote for Christina for Student Council

I would like your vote today so I can help you get what you want out of our school. I will work hard to make Mesa Verde a better place for all of us. Do **you** have good ideas to help our school? Then vote for Christina–Taylor Green

and I will make it happen!

Christina-Taylor with her Little League coaches, Mike Kochanski (left) and John Ward, in the fall of 2010.

Christina and Dallas in Marin County, California, October 2010.

In San Francisco,
October 2010.

Christina-Taylor, John, Dallas,
and me in Tucson, December 2010.

By Jeff Koterba, *Omaha World Herald*

One of two ice sculptures at Christina-Taylor's
funeral reception, January 2011.

The Angel of Steadfast Love sculpture by Lei Hennessy
Owen, installed at Green Field in Tucson, 2011.

The sun brings out the stunning color and detail.

The Christina-Taylor Green Memorial iron-on patch.

9-11-01
CTG
1-8-11

My very good friend Stephanie T. Grandpre was the first person to visit me on 1/8/11. This is her art, based on Christina-Taylor's last drawing.

Never forget

IN MEMORY OF CHRISTINA GREEN HER DREAM WAS PENN STATE

The brick installed in a sidewalk at Penn State early in 2011.

I seek guidance from above at the Tuesday evening, January 11, 2011, Mass for the Healing of Our Community at Saint Odilia's.

This book is dedicated to my
beautiful mother, Yolanda
Segalini. This is a photo of
her in her prime.

vacy, but they want a picture and a statement. How about this one, and I can say something?"

He was referring to one of a foursome of photographs we had hanging in the kitchen, one of me with Christina. I loved the picture, and while I knew it was inappropriate to expect John or me to go out there and say anything, I was grateful that Greg was willing. I'm not the type of person who wants to be on TV. Our previous funerals had been for my mom and my grandparents, and there had been no news associated with those deaths, no national story, no congresswoman who had been the target.

This was huge, I knew, but I did not want to be bombarded by trucks and vans and cameras and microphones. It was just sinking in that I was never going to have my daughter back ever again. I had no interest in going to the site of the shooting to see how it all happened, and I had even less interest in being interviewed just then.

Bless him, Greg pulled himself together and ventured out in his workout clothes and a ball cap, trying to hide his own devastation. Still cameras clicked and video cameras whined as he held up the picture of Christina-Taylor and me, and he asked again that the press respect our privacy. "They will not be coming out," he said, and when asked about his niece, Greg managed, "She was real special and real sweet."

When he got back into the house, he looked as if he'd been in battle.

By dinnertime, others had shown up, including our friends Doug and Katy Martin, the professional singer Christina-Taylor idolized and often sang with at special occasions.

Samantha Carlson, a sixteen-year-old friend of the family who had been Dallas and Christina-Taylor's babysitter at times, was there too. Her parents, Greg and Nancy, are dear friends. Greg would serve as a pallbearer at the funeral, and Nancy was most helpful with food preparation and serving and cleaning. I don't know what we would have done without friends like her.

After John called Bill Hileman to see if he was home from the hospital yet and to get a report on Suzi—she had taken bullets to the abdomen, thigh, and chest but her wounds were not life-threatening—I said we should run a plate of food over to Bill. Samantha immediately volunteered, no doubt having gotten her caring and nurturing qualities from her mom.

Various other friends were in and out that evening, but the rest of the night seemed like a blur. Blessed as we felt to be surrounded by so many caring people, clouding our minds was the stabbing reality of what had happened. I couldn't push it from my mind— not that I really wanted to. But playing over and over in my head was the finality of the surgeon's words and how dumbstruck I had felt when I withstood the full impact of what he was saying. From having desperately kept myself from imagining the worst to finally hearing that Christina-Taylor was gone so rocked me that every time I thought of it, I was stabbed afresh.

I could tell Dallas was suffering from the shock, as John and I were. One by one, our friends began leaving until once again, late at night, it was just the three of us, alone with our debilitating grief. Dallas wasn't clingy, but he often patted John and me on the arm and asked sweetly if we were all right.

When we finally crashed into bed, John and I just lay there weeping for a long time. But you can cry only so much, and then you're spent. I sensed we were each trying to let the other get some much-needed rest, but I could also tell from our breathing that neither of us was drifting off. Soon we began to talk quietly, remembering our angel. There would be precious little sleep that first night. Someone asked if we had been too upset to sleep. *Upset* doesn't begin to describe the ache of the loss we suffered.

~

I must have drifted off briefly just before dawn, because I awoke with the instant jolt of a truth I still wanted to deny. *Things like this don't happen to me, to us. Could it have been just a bad dream?* I rushed to Christina-Taylor's room, hoping and praying I would see her curled in a ball under her covers. But, of course, no.

> *Heather Grant: I had paced around my house all night, not knowing what I would even say when I saw Roxanna and John and Dallas. Later, as my plane was about to land, a paralyzing anxiety came over me and I could not even form a thought. There was no solution for this horror, no comforting words. This wasn't going to go away. It was the most devastating thing a person, a parent, a friend could ever imagine. What was I supposed to say or do?*
>
> *When Hailey and Camden and I got to their home, it was as if a dark cloud hovered. Sadness was everywhere. The kids and I were compelled to just linger in Christina-Taylor's room. It represented so much of her and reminded us of her vibrant life. I debated with myself over whether to even ask, but I suggested to Roxanna that we would be privileged to sleep in Christina's queen size bed that night. Somehow it seemed right to her too. What an honor.*

Christina had always slept with a little stuffed black lab puppy she named Kaya, and Roxanna told Hailey she could take it with her to the services.

I don't know how John and Roxanna have continued to be the strong people that they are, but Christina was the most amazing little girl and, quite obviously, a true reflection of her parents.

They are in my prayers and heart every second of every day. People say that time heals, but I'm not sure a lifetime will ever heal this wound.

Greg was still handling the press outside, and eventually family members and friends would take turns for weeks until we had to get professional help. The crush of the press became a crazy 24/7 marathon.

Greg urged me to start with at least one national interview, because other media outlets could pull quotes from it and not feel as if I had been invisible. I agreed to begin with one for the Fox News network, because I could do it from my home by phone. No one would be invading my house, and I could sit holding my rosary and one of Christina-Taylor's shirts. I prayed I would be able to get through it.

The Fox people were very nice, making the arrangements by phone, and conducting a pre-interview, mostly to determine whether I would be able to make sense on the air. It allowed me to "meet" the interviewer, in this case Gretchen Carlson. We immediately connected because I could tell she was sincerely empathetic, and she too was a mom. In the days that followed, we would be interviewed by

George Stephanopoulos, Anderson Cooper, and several others. John would do the *Today* show from the Westward Look Hotel, where most of the reporters were staying. Every one was hard, even grueling, but we endured for the sake of Christina-Taylor's legacy. We were determined that people get a glimpse of the wonderful little girl we had known for too short a time.

But this was my first, and difficult as it was, Gretchen walked me through it. I was in tears throughout, but I knew it was important to make myself heard and understood, so I fought to keep my composure. Second to wanting my daughter back, I would rather have been in a fetal position unconscious somewhere.

Gretchen asked me to describe my grief and my daughter. I had to say the grief was beyond words, because it truly was. The overwhelming sense of loss so obliterates your thought process that it simply cannot be labeled. As for Christina-Taylor, I was ready for that one. I said she was beautiful and intelligent, a student council representative who was interested in government and politics. "She was a beautiful girl, inside and out," I said.

The toughest phrases to get through—the ones when I really needed a deep breath to articulate the best I could—were, "I just can't even put it into words. I can't express the devastation and hurt and how we were so robbed of our beautiful princess. She was so intelligent, and her light shines on all of us today and forever.

"I just have it in my heart that my angel is in the arms of my mom and my grandmother in heaven. I lost my mom a year ago, so I'm trying to be positive and strong, because that's what Christina would want. At least I can hold on to the nine beautiful years I had with my daughter that some people never experience. I have my faith, my family, and my friends."

I also told Gretchen how the event Christina-Taylor had attended was meant to be a learning experience. That was so like Christina. I know she was excited about a few hours out with a friend, getting pedicures, and doing lunch, but what really drew her to the event was the chance to learn something new and to get to meet a woman she had heard so much about.

We stayed away from watching much of the news, mostly because we didn't want to see the shooter and hear all the controversy surrounding him. I tucked away in a deep part of my heart the fact that who he was and what he was about and whatever his problems were, they were not the issue. I believed that he was crazy, tormented, and determined to create mayhem regardless. That seeing a little girl in the crowd—and he couldn't have avoided seeing her—didn't slow him down a bit, told me all I needed to know about him.

Christina-Taylor was in the wrong place at the wrong time, and my developing some hatred or bitterness or becoming obsessed with the crazy triggerman would do nothing to bring her back. In fact, it could serve only to plant something ugly in my life. Our experience did make me more fervent about gun control, and of course if parole hearings ever came about, I'd force myself to be there and to tell how our family was stripped of its heart.

John is old-school and macho enough to carry the ball on capital punishment. I don't see what would be accomplished by it, and I'd be satisfied to know the man was behind bars for the rest of his life. But, frankly, I find it hard to argue with a loving father who would just as soon see justice fully served.

John: My wife is very forgiving in that regard. I'm a little about the Old West. It's a fairly clear-cut case, and I'm a fan of capital punishment in this circumstance. I wouldn't care to even talk to the guy, because that wouldn't change anything. My daughter's gone and she's not coming back. That would be a waste of breath.

I told Gretchen Carlson that I didn't "really want to say on air what I want to happen to the suspect. It's beyond words. I just want [there to be change] for my little girl, and for everybody involved. I want there to be awareness that these sick people are out there, and this has to stop right now.

"I'm really sorry and devastated about my little girl and all the people who were killed and hurt in this terrible tragedy, but I just hope we can learn from this and gain awareness and make changes so it never happens again."

I did find it heartwarming to see that Christina-Taylor's third grade teacher, Kathie DeKnikker, told the *Washington Post*, "Christina Green was a wonderful child. She had not only the energy and enthusiasm of a typical third-grader, but also maturity and insight that most children don't attain until much later."

Kathie also said that Christina-Taylor had been a leader in her classroom at Mesa Verde Elementary and that she had helped other students and contributed to discussions. "The thing I will remember most about Christina was her well-developed sense of humor. Oh, how she could make us laugh with her witty comments. We will all miss her terribly."

I told the *Arizona Daily Star* that Christina-Taylor "kept up with everyone. She was a strong girl, a very good athlete and a strong swimmer. She was interested in everything. She got a guitar for Christmas, so her next thing was learning to play guitar."

I added that she was "already aware of the inequalities of the world. She often told me, 'We are so blessed. We have the best life.'"

From the Sprint store next to Safeway, employee Jason Pekau hears fifteen to twenty rounds of gunfire. People with bloody clothes run toward him and he sees bodies on the ground.

CHAPTER THIRTEEN

THE OUTPOURING

Tribulation produces perseverance;
and perseverance, character; and
character, hope (Romans 5:3–4).

That second day at home brought more and more friends, and I'm not exaggerating when I say the phone seemed to never stop ringing. You'd hang up from one person and it would ring again immediately. We will never forget the avalanche of love and condolences and support we received from all over.

Everyone who visited our home was so wonderful that I hesitate to single anyone out for fear of shortchanging all the others. But I have to say that when our friends Leslie and Clark Crist arrived with their grown kids Randilyn and Justin, things began to change in a remarkable way. Leslie is a former teacher and principal and now serves as president of San Miguel High School in Tucson. She showed up in teacher/administrator mode, with a notebook and assignments for all. In a friendly, efficient, nonthreatening way, Leslie organized everyone, decreed that neither John nor I would be answering the phone anymore, and assigned that task to various ones in different shifts. It would be hard to overstate what a relief this proved to be. We were nearly beside ourselves, seriously sleep deprived, grieving a loss beyond words, all while worrying about relatives' and friends' flights, where everyone was going to sleep, what to do with all the food, and when people would eat. To basically be told to just stop worrying about all the logistics gave us time and space to breathe.

We still had Christmas decorations that needed to be taken down and a myriad of other little things to be done, knowing that more people were coming and that memorial and funeral arrangements had to be made. How freeing it was to have Leslie just start assigning tasks and establishing rules of practice—what John and I were to do and not do.

Despite the flurry of activity in our home, because of this sudden burst of organizational help, we were freed to start thinking about Christina-Taylor's viewing, funeral, and cremation. Despite our aversion to the news coverage—it was simply too painful to have everything reenacted over and over, plus we wanted to avoid seeing the photos of the shooter and hearing all the details about him—by now we were getting the picture of the carnage beyond our own loss.

Five others had lost their lives in what had become a monstrous national tragedy. How ironic that Christina-Taylor's short life had been bookended by two of the darkest days in American history—starting with the 9/11/01 attacks and ending with this senseless shooting.

The most famous local victim was the Honorable John McCarthy Roll, 63, a federal judge for the United States District Court for the District of Arizona. John Roberts, the chief justice of the U.S. Supreme Court, said, "The violence in Arizona has senselessly taken six lives and inflicted tragic loss on dedicated public servants and their families. We in the judiciary have suffered the terrible loss of one of our own. Chief Judge John Roll was a wise jurist who selflessly served Arizona and the nation with great distinction, as attorney and judge, for more than thirty-five years. I express my deepest condolences to his wife, Maureen, and his children, as well as the other victims and their families. Chief Judge Roll's death is a somber reminder of the importance of the rule of law and the sacrifices of those who work to secure it."

The other victims included:

> Dorothy "Dot" Morris, 76, a retired secretary
> Phyllis Schneck, 79, a homemaker
> Dorwan Stoddard, 76, a retired construction worker
> Gabriel "Gabe" Zimmerman, 30, community outreach
> director for Congresswoman Giffords

~~~

Leslie Crist handled most of Christina-Taylor's funeral arrangements for us too, which was a great help. Fortunately, Katy Martin knew the family who owned one of the oldest funeral parlors in

Tucson, the Brings. As a favor to Katy and to us, they sent Belinda Motzkin-Brauer from their staff to make a rare house call and work with us directly.

Many have told me they wondered why I wasn't catatonic at this point, and naturally I was merely functioning on adrenaline. But I was determined to honor my daughter's legacy. I wanted her funeral to be like that of a princess, because that's what she was to us. In a just world, people all over the country would have known about Christina-Taylor during her life simply because of the dynamic, caring, and talented girl she was. While it was sad that it took her death to give us an opportunity to let others know about her as a real person, I did want as many people as possible to get some idea of how special she was.

Belinda was most compassionate and understanding and walked us through the process at our own pace, listening to the distinct things that would make Christina-Taylor's memorial unique. She worked with our old friends, local businesses, restaurants, and seemingly the whole Tucson community to make sure the funeral would be perfectly appropriate and unforgettable.

We carefully chose the locations of the services. The first of the planned memorials for all the victims would be held on Tuesday evening, January 11, 2011, at our church, St. Odilia's. The next night, January 12, at the same church, there would be a rosary and open-casket viewing of Christina-Taylor. Her funeral was set for 3 p.m. Eastern time, Thursday, January 13, at St. Elizabeth Ann Seton, which could accommodate the huge expected crowd.

To serve as the eight pallbearers, we asked my brothers, Paul and Greg Segalini; John's brother and sister, Doug and Kim Green;

John's sister and brother-in-law, Dana and Mark Ressler; Nancy's husband, Greg Carlson; and Leslie's husband, Clark Crist.

Among the most special contributions to the viewing were ice sculptures created by a local artist that included images of Christina-Taylor—one was of an angel. These were placed in the reception area where people gathered to visit and eat.

We were also thrilled to hear from a group of Roman Catholic monks in Iowa who donated a hand-crafted casket. It would be made by Trappist Caskets, owned by the New Melleray Abbey near Dubuque. The casket would be custom engraved with Christina-Taylor's name and dates of birth and death. The monks also said they would bless it before shipping it to us.

The casket was made of red oak from the monastery's forest, and the monks also made keepsake crosses for our family and said they would plant a red oak tree in Christina's honor in the spring.

We explained to Belinda that we wanted to parcel out Christina-Taylor's ashes so we could spread some over our property, in the yard where my mother had lived, the Maryland farm, Yankee Stadium, Ground Zero, Cape Cod, Boston, and Citizens Bank Park in Philadelphia,where the Phillies play. We kept enough to always have some with us in a beautiful urn in our house, as well as to be able to spread some in the Caribbean she loved so much.

During all this time, while we were trying to ignore the news, friends and relatives filled us in on things they thought we would want to know. We were told of hundreds who had gathered for a vigil at the Arizona Capitol as early as the night of the shootings. We were also told of statements made by Major League Baseball. The owner of the Dodgers, John's employers, said, "We lost a member of the family today. [We] will do everything we can to support John, his wife, Roxanna, and their son, Dallas, in the aftermath of this senseless tragedy."

Jeff Wilpon, the chief operating officer of the New York Mets, whom Christina-Taylor's grandfather had worked for from 1993 through 1996, said, "Our thoughts and condolences go out to Dallas, his wife, Sylvia, the entire Green family, and everybody impacted..."

The former executive director of the Major League Baseball Players Association, Donald Fehr, said, "The loss of anyone in this way, but particularly the loss of a child, simply cannot be excused, minimized, or explained—just condemned."

As you can imagine, Christina-Taylor's grandparents, Nana and Pop Green, were heartbroken. Dallas Green was in his mid-seventies by now but still a gigantic figure in any setting. He's always been known as gruff and straightforward, even verbally sparring with Yankees owner George Steinbrenner back in the day. But this rocked him. Christina had held a special spot in his heart.

Through tears, my father-in-law told reporter Mike Lupica of the *New York Daily News*, "It's hard. We're all hurting pretty bad. I can't believe this could happen to any nine-year-old child, much less our own. This is by far the worst thing to ever happen to us."

Someone on phone duty excitedly told us the White House had called to set up a time the next day for President Obama to speak to us. It was another of those ironies attached to this nightmare. No one in our family had ever even seen a U.S. president, and since my mother and I and my daughter had all been supporters of Obama's, this should have been an honor. And it was. But the price! Had nothing happened to Christina-Taylor, it's likely I could have lived out the rest of my life never having spoken to a president.

And that would have been fine with me. I was touched, of course, that he would be calling, but such a privilege was not worth my loss.

⟍⟋

Needless to say, my pain was still fresh and deep on Monday, January 10, when the president called, so I remember little about the conversation. It had been just over forty-eight hours since we had lost Christina-Taylor, but I do recall that President Obama spoke to me as naturally as if he were a friend or neighbor. He sounded compassionate and humble and admitted that "there simply aren't words to express the pain Michelle and I feel for you and your family. We're so deeply sorry for your loss."

I didn't get the impression this was a prepared speech. He spoke emotionally, from the heart, as a father of two girls. I heard genuineness in his voice. And while he acknowledged that nothing he or anyone else could say or do could make this any easier, I have to say that his call was comforting.

He talked to John and Dallas briefly too, and I think we all felt a little better. Before hanging up, he informed us that he would be speaking at the University of Arizona two days later, Wednesday evening, and invited us to be his personal guests. "I'd like to meet you and have Michelle meet you," he said. "And we can provide seating for as many friends and relatives as you wish."

I told him we really appreciated the invitation, but since that was the evening of Christina-Taylor's viewing, it would be impossible.

"I'm going to see if someone on my staff can arrange to get you here beforehand," he said, "so we can still meet you and then get you back to where you need to be."

I thanked him profusely, doubting if even he could pull that off. Though he would be speaking less than fourteen miles from our home, getting there and back on time during one of the busiest days of our lives seemed out of the question. Even John, a glass-half-full kind of guy, said, "There is just no way. I mean, the traffic when the president comes to town . . ."

But we were soon informed that a car and driver would be provided and that the White House would work with local authorities to guarantee clear sailing there and back in plenty of time for our obligations. I still couldn't imagine it, but you don't turn down an invitation from the president of the United States.

⁓

The next evening, Tuesday, January 11, St. Odilia's hosted the Mass for the Healing of Our Community. The church lies just blocks from my mother's old house and from the shooting scene. Though I had been virtually unable to sleep, and no one else in the family was up to going, I knew I had to find the strength to be there. I had to go to represent my family in the first pew in front of the entire nation. Fortunately, Heather Grant attended with me, along with Leslie, Clark, and Randilyn Crist.

It marked the first time I had left the house since we'd gotten home from the hospital. It seemed so strange to be in public, to know that every eye was on me. I prayed extra hard for God to help me, when I longed to just collapse into bed. As desperately as I wanted to celebrate Christina-Taylor's life, it pierced my soul to be reminded of her death. Grief is a deeply personal and private thing, but I knew friends and even strangers wanted to be there to support us and share in honoring all the victims. Holding my head up and trying to maintain my composure was the hardest work I've ever done.

The sanctuary seats 700, and it was full. More people watched on a monitor in the parish hall. Judge Roll's family was there, as was Bill Badger, the retired Army colonel who tackled the shooter, and members of Gabe Zimmerman's family.

People of all faiths had gathered to comfort each other, and the beautiful service was officiated by the Most Reverend Gerald Kicanas, bishop of the Tucson Diocese, and several other local religious leaders. I know my mom was with me that evening. The bishop reassured the crowd that God had not abandoned us—that He "stands by us, walks with us, and holds us in the palm of His hand. . . . I know Christina is with us and that God has welcomed home all six victims."

The night was chilly as we exited the church, but my heart was warm from the beautiful service about forgiveness and healing. And I was especially encouraged by our own Father Richard Troutman of St. Odilia's, who took my hand and whispered that I was the "rock of the family."

I needed to hear that. I didn't feel like a rock just then, but I am strong. John is strong enough to speak in public, but behind the scenes, like most moms, I keep things going, comforting others and stepping up when everyone else throws in the towel. That Father Troutman knew this about me and said so meant the world to me during a very dark time. He made me feel better and gave me strength to get through the next few difficult days of services.

On the front page of the paper the next day there was a big photo of Heather, Leslie, and me in that front pew. I had my eyes closed with my face turned toward heaven.

Wednesday, January 12, was another whirlwind day. People were calling, and coming and going from the house, and we were trying to prepare ourselves for Christina-Taylor's viewing that night—after getting to the University of Arizona to meet the president and first lady and, hopefully, getting back in time.

I needn't have worried. The White House and the local authorities worked together to block off streets and create an unobstructed path for our limousine and escort vehicles. We flew there as if we were in an Indy 500 car. We were delivered to the massive McKale Memorial Center, where the Arizona Wildcats play basketball in an arena that holds more than 14,000 people. It would be full that night for "Together We Thrive: Tucson and America," highlighted by the president's speech.

Security shuffled John and Dallas and me into a side room where we were to wait for the president and his wife. Former Supreme Court Justice Sandra Day O'Connor—who was the first woman on the high court and who served nearly fifteen years before stepping down five years earlier—came in with Justice Anthony Kennedy. I recognized senators and local politicians and often found myself wondering, *Is that who I think it is?*

The dignitaries greeted us and extended their condolences, and we got to meet Kelly, the fiancée of one of the other victims, Gabe Zimmerman, along with Judge Roll's widow, whom I found amazing. She seemed so brave and strong. She had been quoted, "There are no words to describe how my world was shattered Saturday morning. Not only did I lose my husband and best friend of more than forty years, but our three sons lost a wonderful father and our grandchildren their beloved Papa."

Yet she was worried about me. She said, "John lived his life and accomplished just about everything he set out to do. But you lost your child." I found it remarkable that she cared so much during her own grief.

I expected the president to have a big entourage, but apparently his Secret Service detail just escorted him to the door and remained outside. Wearing a dark suit with a blue tie, he entered with Michelle, who wore a plum skirt, black top, and a light, white sweater.

They came directly to John, Dallas, and me and embraced us all. Again the president mentioned that as the parent of daughters, he couldn't imagine how we were suffering. He and Michelle once again expressed their sorrow over our loss.

Dallas had drawn a picture of a dinosaur for them, and they really responded with enthusiasm. President Obama said, "This is great!"

Michelle asked Dallas if he wanted to meet the girls, but as soon as she saw his shy reaction, she said, "Oh, that's okay, Dallas. You're probably not into girls right now. But you'll have to come to the White House sometime and meet Bo, the dog. Would you like that?"

"Oh, yeah, I'd love that!"

I so appreciated the first lady making Dallas feel comfortable.

Soon it was time for the president to prepare for his speech and for us to get back on the road to Christina-Taylor's viewing. Nothing else would have kept us from that speech that night. And from what I heard about the tributes to the wounded, the dead, the heroes, and the emergency personnel, I wish we could have stayed. I saw a piece of the president's speech and have to say that even those who are not fans of Mr. Obama consider it one of his finest hours.

Here, in its entirety, is the speech he gave that night, capping off an emotional memorial:

> To the families of those we've lost; to all who called them friends; to the students of this university, the public servants who are gathered here, the people of Tucson, and the people of Arizona: I have come here tonight as an American who, like all Americans, kneels to pray with you today and will stand by you tomorrow.
>
> There is nothing I can say that will fill the sudden hole torn in your hearts. But know this: The hopes of a nation are here tonight. We mourn with you for the fallen. We join you in your grief. And we add our faith to yours that Representative Gabrielle Giffords and the other living victims of this tragedy will pull through.
>
> Scripture tells us:
> *There is a river whose streams make glad the city of God,*
> *the holy place where the Most High dwells.*
> *God is within her, she will not fall;*
> *God will help her at break of day.*
>
> On Saturday morning, Gabby, her staff, and many of her constituents gathered outside a supermarket to exercise their right to peaceful assembly and free speech. They were fulfilling a central tenet of the democracy envisioned by our founders—representatives of the people

answering questions to their constituents, so as to carry their concerns back to our nation's capital. Gabby called it "Congress on Your Corner"—just an updated version of government of and by and for the people.

And that quintessentially American scene, that was the scene that was shattered by a gunman's bullets. And the six people who lost their lives on Saturday—they, too, represented what is best in us, what is best in America.

Judge John Roll served our legal system for nearly forty years. A graduate of this university and a graduate of this law school, Judge Roll was recommended for the federal bench by John McCain twenty years ago, appointed by President George H. W. Bush, and rose to become Arizona's chief federal judge.

His colleagues described him as the hardest-working judge within the Ninth Circuit. He was on his way back from attending Mass, as he did every day, when he decided to stop by and say hi to his representative. John is survived by his loving wife, Maureen, his three sons, and his five beautiful grandchildren.

George and Dorothy Morris—"Dot" to her friends—were high school sweethearts who got married and had two daughters. They did everything together—traveling the open road in their RV, enjoying what their friends called a fifty-year honeymoon. Saturday morning, they went by the Safeway to hear what their congresswoman had to say. When gunfire rang out, George, a former Marine, instinctively tried to shield his wife. Both were shot. Dot passed away.

A New Jersey native, Phyllis Schneck retired to Tucson to beat the snow. But in the summer, she would return East, where her world revolved around her three children, her seven grandchildren, and two-year-old great-granddaughter. A gifted quilter, she'd often work under a favorite tree, or sometimes she'd sew aprons with the logos of the Jets and the Giants to give out at the church where she volunteered. A Republican, she took a liking to Gabby and wanted to get to know her better.

Dorwan and Mavy Stoddard grew up in Tucson together—about seventy years ago. They moved apart and started their own respective families. But after both were widowed, they found their way back here to, as one of Mavy's daughters put it, "be boyfriend and girlfriend again."

When they weren't out on the road in their motor home, you could find them just up the road, helping folks in need at the Mountain Avenue Church of Christ. A retired construction worker, Dorwan spent his spare time fixing up the church along with his dog, Tux. His final act of selflessness was to dive on top of his wife, sacrificing his life for hers.

Everything—everything—Gabe Zimmerman did, he did with passion. But his true passion was helping people. As Gabby's outreach director, he made the cares of thousands of her constituents his own, seeing to it that seniors got the Medicare benefits that they had earned, that veterans got the medals and the care that they deserved, that government was working for ordinary folks. He died doing what he loved—talking with people and seeing how he could help. And Gabe is survived by his parents, Ross and Emily, his brother, Ben, and his fiancée, Kelly, who he planned to marry next year.

And then there is nine-year-old Christina-Taylor Green. Christina was an A student; she was a dancer; she was a gymnast; she was a swimmer. She decided that she wanted to be the first woman to play in the major leagues, and as the only girl on her Little League team, no one put it past her.

She showed an appreciation for life uncommon for a girl her age. She'd remind her mother, "We are so blessed. We have the best life." And she'd pay those blessings back by participating in a charity that helped children who were less fortunate.

Our hearts are broken by their sudden passing. Our hearts are broken—and yet, our hearts also have reason for fullness.

Our hearts are full of hope and thanks for the thirteen Americans who survived the shooting, including the congresswoman many of them went to see on Saturday.

I have just come from the University Medical Center, just a mile from here, where our friend Gabby courageously fights to recover even as we speak. And I want to tell you—her husband, Mark, is here and he allows me to share this with you—right after we went to visit, a few minutes after we left her room and some of her colleagues in Congress were in the room, Gabby opened her eyes for the first time. Gabby opened her eyes for the first time.

Gabby opened her eyes. Gabby opened her eyes, so I

can tell you she knows we are here. She knows we love her. And she knows that we are rooting for her through what is undoubtedly going to be a difficult journey. We are there for her.

Our hearts are full of thanks for that good news, and our hearts are full of gratitude for those who saved others. We are grateful to Daniel Hernandez, a volunteer in Gabby's office.

And, Daniel, I'm sorry—you may deny it—but we've decided you are a hero because you ran through the chaos to minister to your boss, and tended to her wounds and helped keep her alive.

We are grateful to the men who tackled the gunman as he stopped to reload. Right over there. We are grateful for petite Patricia Maisch, who wrestled away the killer's ammunition and undoubtedly saved some lives. And we are grateful for the doctors and nurses and first responders who worked wonders to heal those who'd been hurt. We are grateful to them.

These men and women remind us that heroism is found not only on the fields of battle. They remind us that heroism does not require special training or physical strength. Heroism is here, in the hearts of so many of our fellow citizens all around us, just waiting to be summoned—as it was on Saturday morning. Their actions, their selflessness poses a challenge to each of us. It raises a question of what, beyond prayers and expressions of concern, is required of us going forward. How can we honor the fallen? How can we be true to their memory?

You see, when a tragedy like this strikes, it is part of our nature to demand explanations—to try and [im]pose some order on the chaos and make sense out of that which seems senseless. Already we've seen a national conversation commence, not only about the motivations behind these killings, but about everything from the merits of gun safety laws to the adequacy of our mental health system. And much of this process, of debating what might be done to prevent such tragedies in the future, is an essential ingredient in our exercise of self-government.

But at a time when our discourse has become so sharply polarized—at a time when we are far too eager to lay the blame for all that ails the world at the feet of those who happen to think differently than we do—it's important for us to pause for a moment and make sure that we're talking with each other in a way that heals, not in a way that wounds.

Scripture tells us that there is evil in the world, and that terrible things happen for reasons that defy human understanding. In the words of Job, "When I looked for light, then came darkness." Bad things happen, and we have to guard against simple explanations in the aftermath.

For the truth is, none of us can know exactly what triggered this vicious attack. None of us can know with any certainty what might have stopped these shots from being fired, or what thoughts lurked in the inner recesses of a violent man's mind. Yes, we have to examine all the facts behind this tragedy. We cannot and will not be passive in the face of such violence. We should be willing to

challenge old assumptions in order to lessen the prospects of such violence in the future. But what we cannot
do is use this tragedy as one more occasion to turn on
each other. That we cannot do. That we cannot do.

As we discuss these issues, let each of us do so with
a good dose of humility. Rather than pointing fingers
or assigning blame, let's use this occasion to expand our
moral imaginations, to listen to each other more carefully, to sharpen our instincts for empathy and remind
ourselves of all the ways that our hopes and dreams are
bound together.

After all, that's what most of us do when we lose somebody in our family—especially if the loss is unexpected.
We're shaken out of our routines. We're forced to look
inward. We reflect on the past: Did we spend enough
time with an aging parent? we wonder. Did we express
our gratitude for all the sacrifices that they made for us?
Did we tell a spouse just how desperately we loved them,
not just once in a while but every single day?

So sudden loss causes us to look backward—but it also
forces us to look forward; to reflect on the present and
the future, on the manner in which we live our lives and
nurture our relationships with those who are still with us.

We may ask ourselves if we've shown enough kindness and generosity and compassion to the people in our
lives. Perhaps we question whether we're doing right by
our children or our community—whether our priorities
are in order.

We recognize our own mortality, and we are reminded that in the fleeting time we have on this earth, what matters is not wealth, or status, or power, or fame—but rather, how well we have loved and what small part we have played in making the lives of other people better.

And that process—that process of reflection, of making sure we align our values with our actions—that, I believe, is what a tragedy like this requires.

For those who were harmed, those who were killed—they are part of our family, an American family 300 million strong. We may not have known them personally, but surely we see ourselves in them. In George and Dot, in Dorwan and Mavy, we sense the abiding love we have for our own husbands, our own wives, our own life partners. Phyllis—she's our mom or our grandma; Gabe—our brother or son. In Judge Roll, we recognize not only a man who prized his family and doing his job well, but also a man who embodied America's fidelity to the law.

And in Gabby—in Gabby—we see a reflection of our public-spiritedness; that desire to participate in that sometimes frustrating, sometimes contentious, but always necessary and never-ending process to form a more perfect union.

And in Christina—in Christina—we see all of our children. So curious, so trusting, so energetic, so full of magic. So deserving of our love. And so deserving of our good example.

If this tragedy prompts reflection and debate—as it should—let's make sure it's worthy of those we have lost.

Let's make sure it's not on the usual plane of politics and point-scoring and pettiness that drifts away in the next news cycle.

The loss of these wonderful people should make every one of us strive to be better. To be better in our private lives, to be better friends and neighbors and coworkers and parents. And if, as has been discussed in recent days, their death helps usher in more civility in our public discourse, let us remember it is not because a simple lack of civility caused this tragedy—it did not—but rather because only a more civil and honest public discourse can help us face up to the challenges of our nation in a way that would make them proud.

We should be civil because we want to live up to the example of public servants like John Roll and Gabby Giffords, who knew first and foremost that we are all Americans; and that we can question each other's ideas without questioning each other's love of country; and that our task, working together, is to constantly widen the circle of our concern so that we bequeath the American Dream to future generations.

They believed—they believed, and I believe—that we can be better. Those who died here, those who saved life here—they help me believe. We may not be able to stop all evil in the world, but I know that how we treat one another, that's entirely up to us.

And I believe that for all our imperfections, we are full of decency and goodness, and that the forces that divide us are not as strong as those that unite us.

That's what I believe, in part because that's what a child like Christina-Taylor Green believed.

Imagine—imagine for a moment—here was a young girl who was just becoming aware of our democracy; just beginning to understand the obligations of citizenship; just starting to glimpse the fact that some day she, too, might play a part in shaping her nation's future. She had been elected to her student council. She saw public service as something exciting and hopeful. She was off to meet her congresswoman, someone she was sure was good and important and might be a role model. She saw all this through the eyes of a child, undimmed by the cynicism or vitriol that we adults all too often just take for granted.

I want to live up to her expectations. I want our democracy to be as good as Christina imagined it. I want America to be as good as she imagined it. All of us—we should do everything we can to make sure this country lives up to our children's expectations.

As has already been mentioned, Christina was given to us on September 11th, 2001, one of fifty babies born that day to be pictured in a book called *Faces of Hope*. On either side of her photo in that book were simple wishes for a child's life. "I hope you help those in need," read one. "I hope you know all the words to the National Anthem and sing it with your hand over your heart. . . . I hope you jump in rain puddles."

If there are rain puddles in heaven, Christina is jumping in them today. And here on this earth—here on this earth—we place our hands over our hearts, and we commit ourselves as Americans to forging a country that is forever worthy of her gentle, happy spirit.

May God bless and keep those we've lost in restful and eternal peace. May He love and watch over the survivors. And may He bless the United States of America.[1]

The first of many 9-1-1 calls is received about the shooting. Immediately after, two men tackle the shooter and hold him until police arrive.

CHAPTER FOURTEEN

IN REMEMBRANCE

THE FRUIT OF THE SPIRIT IS LOVE, JOY,
PEACE, LONGSUFFERING, KINDNESS,
GOODNESS, FAITHFULNESS, GENTLENESS, SELF
CONTROL (GALATIANS 5:22–23).

President Obama's speech that Wednesday night was powerful stuff. I thought he did a wonderful job, and it was obvious to all that the youngest victim of the horrible ordeal had affected him not only as a president, but also as a father. When a man in his position says he wants all of us to live up to Christina-Taylor's expectations of this country, that tells me she's made an impact not only in Tucson, but also all over the country. I couldn't have been more proud.

While he was speaking at the University of Arizona, we were at Christina-Taylor's viewing at St. Odilia's. I was stunned at the massive security detail that had been assigned to the church, including a SWAT team. I was told that authorities were worried about copycat crazies who might want to duplicate the horror of four days before.

We had also heard that the infamous Westboro Baptist Church of Topeka, Kansas, planned to prey on the funerals of the six victims of the Tucson shootings. Their *modus operandi* is to picket such funerals and those of slain American soldiers, carrying signs that say that God hates homosexuals and that our war deaths are evidence of His judgment on America.

I believe in the freedom of speech, even when it allows hate-mongers to say horrible things, but I've never been able to understand the motive behind these people or to justify the pain they inflict on already-grieving people.

The last thing I wanted was for them to show up at any type of memorial for Christina-Taylor or any of the other victims. And I confess I was pleased when I heard what happened when they originally announced their plans. They had said they were going to taunt mourners at the funerals and that they would also demonstrate at the intersection near the Safeway where the massacre took place.

Locals responded immediately by planning what they called an "angel action." People dressed as angels and wearing gigantic wings would block the Westboro people from view. And Arizona politicians quickly passed a bill to prohibit the Westboro representatives from coming within 300 feet of any of the funerals.

"Such despicable acts of emotional terrorism will not be toler-ated in the State of Arizona," Governor Jan Brewer said. "This leg-islation will assure that the victims of Saturday's tragic shooting in Tucson will be laid to rest in peace with the full dignity and respect that they deserve."

Still, I didn't want them there at all, of course, and I was pleased to see no sign of them when we arrived at St. Odilia's for the view-ing on Wednesday evening, the night before Christina-Taylor's funeral. I soon learned that Westboro had announced they would not appear at her viewing or funeral in exchange for time on radio stations in Toronto and Phoenix a week after the shootings. I wasn't excited about their getting any publicity or a chance to spread their hatred, but this was sure better than the alternative. They could exercise their freedom of speech, and listeners could exercise their option to turn off their radios.

At the viewing, where about a quarter of the attendance was made up of children—Little Leaguers, classmates, kids from church, and strangers—a woman approached John and me and asked if she could share something with us. As we stood near Christina-Taylor's casket, which sat next to an altar lined with red, white, pink, and yellow flow-ers, she said, "You don't know me, but my son is new to Mesa Verde this year and sat on the bus all alone for the first few weeks. Some kids were making fun of him, and he was unhappy and not feeling welcome. Well, your daughter noticed this, and for two weeks she sat with him and talked with him all the way to school, making him feel much better. Ever since then, he has adjusted well, plays with the other kids, and is happy at school. I just wanted to thank you and let you know she made a big impact on my son. She was quite a girl."

We thanked her and couldn't hold back our tears. Christina-Taylor had never mentioned that to either of us, but the story was yet another glimpse into the type of person she was.

Hailey Grant, the eleven-year-old daughter of my best friend and Christina-Taylor's godmother, Heather Grant, recently sent me her memories of their visit for the viewing and funeral:

> My best friend Christina was in a horrible tragedy in Tucson, Arizona, January 8, 2011. After she died some of her organs went to a girl in Boston and saved her life, and Christina's corneas allowed another child to see.
>
> The last time I saw Christina was in October 2010, and I was so happy. Our moms are best friends, so we saw each other a couple of times a year. We always talked about boys and always gave each other makeovers.
>
> During her family's visit here, we went to San Francisco, and her uncle Paul came to meet up with us and we all watched the Blue Angels. We had the best time of our lives. When she had to go back home and I said good-bye, I didn't realize that good-bye really meant good-bye.
>
> After I heard about the tragedy I burst into tears and didn't understand why God would let this happen. My brother and I went to Tucson with my mom, and my godmother, Roxanna, was all dressed up because she was about to meet the president of the United States.
>
> That night was also the viewing. I had never been to a viewing before. I was in the second group to see Christina.

I walked in holding her stuffed dog Kaya that she has had since she was a baby. I was crying so much, I was screaming inside.

Christina was beautiful, wearing her diamond crown from her First Communion and her Christmas dress. I was supposed to put in her stuffed Kaya next to her but instead I gave it to my godfather, John, and he put it in Christina's arm. I was crying so hard I couldn't stop. Finally I knelt and prayed, then said my final good-bye, but I couldn't leave. It was impossible for me. I was still screaming inside and totally crying—it was just horrible.

We still think about Christina and pray for her every day. She was my best friend and will be in my heart forever.

⌒

Christina-Taylor's funeral—the first of the six resulting from the shooting rampage—was scheduled for three o'clock in the afternoon, Eastern time, Thursday, January 13, 2011. That was one o'clock our time, and it had been just five days since we'd lost her. Despite all the activity that had been packed into those few days, something about getting ready to go to the actual funeral had such a sense of finality about it that I had to force myself through every step.

That morning former Supreme Court Justice Sandra Day O'Connor, whom we had seen the afternoon before at the McHale Center, released a statement about the shootings:

As we grieve, we must not allow these events to further divide our state and our nation. We must reject violence and hostility and bring civility and rational dialogue into our government and our community life. This is a responsibility of every one of us as individuals. Only we—working together—can restore reason and civility in our public speech and actions.

Congresswoman Giffords is a fine example of a public official who brings these efforts and qualities to her meetings and gatherings. May her health be restored and may we all remember the role each of us plays in restoring civil talk to our public expressions.

Before speaking out, ask yourself whether your words are true, whether they are respectful, and whether they are needed in our civil discussions.

⌒

I knew Christina-Taylor's funeral would be special, but I would have given anything for it not to have been necessary. If ever there would be a final good-bye, this would be it. I wanted to do what Christina-Taylor would want me to do, what would make her proud and happy. I look at pictures of myself that day and see a drawn, hollow-faced, grieving mother, struggling to honor her daughter. Sometimes I wonder how I got through it, but I know God was with me and sent hundreds of friends and loved ones and supporters to help give me strength.

Once our family was dressed and ready, the cars and limos began lining up outside our home. Normally when something like that happens, it's for a festive time—a party or a prom or a wedding. This, of course, was anything but festive. I kept telling myself that it was not about us; it was about Christina-Taylor, and as much as I hated to have to endure it, I wanted everything to be perfect.

It was so surreal to start loading up family and friends for the procession to the church, less than two miles away. The somber convoy slowly made its way north up sloping North Shannon Road toward the quiet, desert adobe St. Elizabeth Ann Seton Church, tucked into the foothills of the Santa Catalina Mountains.

I was stunned to see the streets lined for the last quarter mile with more than a thousand people flanked on both sides. Among them were the eighteen volunteer angels, dressed in white and bearing seven-foot-tall wings made of plastic pipe and bed sheets. They stood side by side in silence a block from the church, and I was told they stayed there for an hour and a half.

Others in the crowd were dressed in baseball uniforms, some carrying teddy bears or bouquets. People of all ages, some in genuine cowboy regalia, stood side by side. Signs were everywhere, expressing love for Christina-Taylor and pleading for an end to hate and violence.

As we neared the church we found 200 motorcycles lined up, engines off and silent, their riders saluting.

A makeshift arch had been erected over the entrance to the church by two gigantic hook and ladder fire trucks. Their ladders extended to support a forty-five-pound, twenty-by-thirty-foot American flag that had been salvaged from Ground Zero, where the World Trade Center twin towers had stood until Christina-Taylor's birthday, September 11, 2001. The massive banner had been flying at 90 West Street in New York when the towers went down. Pieces of flags from all fifty states had been used to patch it, and it was personally delivered to the church by members of the New York Says Thank You Foundation. There was something quietly, majestically thrilling about it.

Our large contingent of family and dear friends disembarked from the limos and gathered beneath that flag, holding hands, weeping, and pausing for a moment of silence. When the hearse arrived and the beautifully handcrafted but painfully small casket emerged, John and Dallas and I gathered behind it and our beloved pallbearers.

Accompanied by white-gloved state troopers, we were escorted inside. The unspeakably painful final good-bye had begun.

The church was decorated with pink flowers and large photos of Christina-Taylor at her smiling, youthful best. She looked so happy, so vibrant, so alive.

We made our way to a private room for just our party. Congresswoman Gabrielle Giffords' husband, the astronaut Mark E. Kelly, came in to pay his respects. He was there with several family members, including his wife's sister. She pressed into my hand a silver saint charm that Gabby and her mother had purchased in Spain. "Gabby wants you to have this."

Mark embraced us and said, "I'm so sorry. Please accept my deepest condolences."

We found him most pleasant and kind, especially considering the strain he was under. We told him we would be praying for Gabby and how pleased we were to hear that she had opened her eyes for the first time the day before.

Dallas and Hailey and Camden Grant got to meet him. Hailey told me later, "He was so nice and is going on his last mission this year, but we didn't talk about that."

Later, as we entered the sanctuary, packed with nearly two thousand people, I was struck that it looked like a state funeral. We saw rows of politicians and dignitaries—including Arizona senators John McCain and Jon Kyl—as well as law enforcement officers in their dress uniforms, and I couldn't help but remember the funeral Christina-Taylor had promised me the day we watched Ted Kennedy's service on TV.

The University of Arizona choir was singing "Ave Maria" in Latin:

> *Ave Maria,*
> *Gratia plena,*
> *Dominus tecum.*
> *Benedicta tu in mulieribus,*
> *Et benedictus fructus ventris tui,*
> *Jesus.*
>
> *Sancta Maria,*
> *Mater Dei,*
> *Ora pro nobis peccatoribus,*
> *Nunc et in hora mortis nostrae.*
> *Amen.*[1]

English translation:

> *Hail Mary,*
> *Full of grace,*
> *The Lord is with thee.*
> *Blessed art thou among women,*
> *And blessed is the fruit of thy womb,*
> *Jesus.*

Holy Mary,
Mother of God,
Pray for us sinners,
Now and at the hour of our death.
Amen.

Other hymns were sung, and there were readings from both the Old and New Testaments.

Psalm 23

The LORD is my shepherd; I shall not want. He makes me to lie down in green pastures; He leads me beside the still waters. He restores my soul; He leads me in the paths of righteousness for His name's sake.

Yea, though I walk through the valley of the shadow of death, I will fear no evil; for You are with me; Your rod and Your staff, they comfort me.

You prepare a table before me in the presence of my enemies; You anoint my head with oil; my cup runs over.

Surely goodness and mercy shall follow me all the days of my life; and I will dwell in the house of the LORD forever.

John 14:1-6

"Let not your heart be troubled; you believe in God, believe also in Me. In My Father's house are many mansions; if it were not so, I would have told you. I go to prepare a place for you. And if I go and prepare a place for you, I will come again and receive you to Myself; that where I am, there you may be also. And where I go you know, and the way you know."

Thomas said to Him, "Lord, we do not know where You are going, and how can we know the way?"

Jesus said to him, "I am the way, the truth, and the life. No one comes to the Father except through Me."

Then, with her husband, Doug, at the piano, my friend Katy—who so loved Christina-Taylor—sang both "Amazing Grace" and Billy Joel's "Lullaby." Many wondered if she would be able to get through the songs, as close as she'd been to Christina, but I knew she'd nail it because she's such a pro. And she did.

"Amazing Grace"
Amazing grace, how sweet the sound,
That saved a wretch like me!
I once was lost, but now am found,
Was blind, but now I see.

'Twas grace that taught my heart to fear,
And grace my fears relieved.
How precious did that grace appear
The hour I first believed.
Through many dangers, toils, and snares
I have already come;
'Tis grace has brought me safe thus far
and grace will lead me home.

The Lord has promised good to me,
His word my hope secures;
He will my shield and portion be,
As long as life endures.

Yea, when this flesh and heart shall fail,
And mortal life shall cease,
I shall possess, within the veil,
A life of joy and peace.

When we've been there ten thousand years,
Bright shining as the sun,
We've no less days to sing God's praise
Than when we first begun.[2]

"Lullaby (Good Night, My Angel)"
Good night, my angel, time to close your eyes
And save these questions for another day.
I think I know what you've been asking me;
I think you know what I've been trying to say.

I promised I would never leave you,
And you should always know,
Wherever you may go,
No matter where you are,
I never will be far away.

Good night, my angel, now it's time to sleep,
And still so many things I want to say.
Remember all the songs you sang for me
When we went sailing on an emerald bay.

And like a boat out on the ocean,
I'm rocking you to sleep.
The water's dark and deep
Inside this ancient heart.
You'll always be a part of me.

Goodnight, my angel, now it's time to dream
And dream how wonderful your life will be.
Someday your child may cry, and if you sing this lullaby,
Then in your heart there will always be a part of me.

Someday we'll all be gone,
But lullabies go on and on.
They never die; that's how you and I will be.[3]

Later we got this note:

Dear John and Roxanna—

I was so deeply touched that my song "Lullaby (Goodnight, My Angel)" was a part of the funeral service for your daughter, Christina. My deepest sympathy goes out to you and your family in this sad time.

The nation's heart is broken. Her birth and death have irrevocably changed us. She will be cherished through all time.

I mourn with you.

Billy Joel[4]

At 10:14 a.m., Saturday, January 8, 2011, the first medical unit, Rural Metro Fire Rescue 76, is dispatched to the scene.

CHAPTER FIFTEEN

FINAL FAREWELL

To everything there is a season,
a time for every purpose under heaven:
a time to be born, and a time to die;
a time to plant, and a time to pluck what is planted;
a time to kill, and a time to heal;
a time to break down, and a time to build up;
a time to weep, and a time to laugh;
a time to mourn, and a time to dance;
a time to cast away stones, and a time to gather stones;
a time to embrace, and a time to refrain from embracing;
a time to gain, and a time to lose;
a time to keep, and a time to throw away;
a time to tear, and a time to sew;
a time to keep silence, and a time to speak;
a time to love, and a time to hate;
a time of war, and a time of peace (Ecclesiastes 3:1–8).

I was so proud of John at the funeral. He did something I never could have done. He had spent hours preparing a eulogy for Christina-Taylor. I don't know how he was able to deliver it without completely falling apart, as I would have done. I had enough memories and reflections to have been able to speak about my daughter for hours, but I wouldn't have been able to finish a sentence.

But big John, who had always been more comfortable in a baseball uniform or casual clothes, looked handsome up there in a nice suit, and somehow held himself together.

He began, "Christina-Taylor Green, I can't tell you how much we all miss you already. I remember you and your brother running around frog ponds, picking blackberries, racing up and down hills in Maryland. There was always laughter.

"In West Grove, Pennsylvania, I can still see you with all the neighborhood kids, sledding in the winter. Of course, you'd be giving all the directions."

Then John looked up at the rapt crowd. "I do know she's affected a lot of people in Tucson, and we are very proud to be members of this community. Just looking around us, we know that we have people here who loved her and love her family. I want you to know that everybody is going to be okay. She would want that.

"In Arizona she took walks in the desert with her grandmother. In the Canyon Del Oro Little League she was quite a competitor. One thing I'll miss is coming home from two weeks of baseball scouting on the road and walking in the door to find my wife and my daughter dressed to the nines and dancing around the house. That's something she loved to do with her mother.

"And her brother, Dallas. They loved snorkeling. They loved swimming together. They were best buddies."

John looked tearfully at his son. "You'll always have your sister here with you, Dallas. She loves you very much."

He turned back to the red oak casket. "Christina, this is a terrible tragedy for all of us. You are familiar with that. You were born on 9/11. You've been through this before. I think you've affected the whole country. We'll never forget you."

John fell silent for a moment and pulled out another sheet of paper. "We have so many people to thank for their support, but one friend, Allan Ford, sent a poem that sums up the way I feel."

> *Tiny angel, can you tell me, why have you gone away?*
> *You weren't here for very long. Why is it you couldn't stay?*
> *Tiny angel shook her head, "These things I do not know.*
> *"But I do know that you love me, and that I love you so."*

John looked exhausted when he rejoined me. He whispered, "I only said about a fourth of what I wrote."

"You were fine," I said. "You did an amazing job."

I think he was planning on reading everything he had written, but when he got up there and teared up, his notes went blurry and he just spoke from his heart. It turns out it wasn't a speech but a father talking to and about his daughter. He made her real to everyone.

⌒

Finally, the Most Reverend Gerald Kicanas, Bishop of the Tucson Diocese—who had returned early from a trip to the Holy Land in time for Christina-Taylor's Tuesday memorial service—preached the homily. It concluded the most beautiful funeral I had ever attended.

He said:

Christina-Taylor Green calls us together this afternoon. This is her celebration. She centers our attention. She stands before us, speaks to us, a child teaches us about the Kingdom of God. This is her appointed time, her time to speak, like when the young Christ stood up in the temple and opened the scroll; we now listen in silence and awe, amazed as her life speaks to us.

Her time to be born was the tragic day of 9/11/2001. Her time to die was the tragic day of January 8, 2011. Just nine years old. Christina found her dwelling place in God's mansion. She went home.

For sure, Christina had her time to laugh, her time to dance, which she loved so much. She had her time to embrace and her time to sow. She had her time to love, and her time to build.

She had her time to outshine the boys in baseball— not softball, but real baseball. She was the best hitter in the league; after all, her grandpa pitched in the major leagues and managed the World Series champion Phillies, and her dad is a Major League Baseball scout. John knew her skill. She had her time to root for the Dodgers and even the Phillies.

She had her time to hug her little black stuffed dog, to love animals, to swim with her brother Dallas, which she so enjoyed. She had her time to model, to be in fashion. She had her time to be elected to the student council, to be a leader, to represent others.

Now is her time to speak.

Christina, just a little girl, holds the wisdom of a wise woman. She wanted to make a difference with her life, to make her mark. She has done so in such a powerful way that even she could not have imagined.

She would want to say to us today, "Love life. Live it to the full. Life, you see, is a gift from God. Don't squander it, waste it, throw it away. Rather, enjoy it. Share it. Make the most of it."

She would want to say to us today, "God has loved me so much, placed His hand on me, and prepared a place with Him for me. This life does not last forever, so don't spend it gathering and accumulating, possessing and owning, being jealous and envious. Rather, seek out ways to help others, to serve others, to make things better for others. That life merits eternal life."

Christina, such a beautiful girl, would want to say to all her friends from Mesa Verde Elementary School, "Here's the baton. Now you run with it. Be great. Do great things." And to her choir friends she would say, "Make beautiful music to praise the Lord. You guys are good, but let me tell you, the heavenly choir is fabulous."

She would want to say, "I love you, Mom and Dad and my brother Dallas. I love you, Grandpa Dallas and Grandma Sylvia. I love all my uncles and aunts and cousins. I know this is a time for you to mourn and a time to cry, but I am okay. Let me tell you, I am in my Father's house with Grandma Yolanda. God wanted me home. I am okay."

That dreadful Saturday morning, Christina went to meet and greet Gabby, her congresswoman, her model and exemplar; instead she met God, her Father, Christ Jesus, her Friend.

"You shall above all things be glad and young. For if you're young, whatever life you wear, it will become you; and if you are glad, whatever's living will yourself become" (E. E. Cummings).

Christina-Taylor Green is young and glad, and to such as these belongs the Kingdom of God.

⁓

The sanctuary was silent and full of emotion when the bagpiper stepped into place and the coffin was situated for the recessional. To the haunting strains of "Amazing Grace," John and Dallas and I fell in behind, and as we moved down the aisle, Dallas laid his hand gently on the casket.

As the crowd followed and we gathered for the reception, John and I were inundated by a long line of guests for nearly the next two hours. We knew we should eat, and we tried, but it was impossible with so many kind people to talk to. Christina-Taylor's classmates and teachers were all there, along with hundreds and hundreds of other friends.

We thanked each one for being strong and brave and for coming to the service, and we told them that Christina was in heaven now.

I said, "Though we're sad, we know she's happy now to be there with God."

Christina-Taylor's best friend Serenity was very emotional and having a most difficult time. She told me how much she loved and missed Christina. Later she gave me this letter she had written:

Memory Book / Christina & Serenity bffs (best friends forever)

Christina, you are my heartbeat that keeps me going, and you were like a sister to me. You even looked like me. EVERYTHING was just right about you.

The memories in first grade, I still remember . . .

I also remember how you loved my dog, Santini. Oh, how you played with him when we had sleepovers at your house! Everything was funner . . .

I enjoyed watching you dance and sing. I'm glad I met you, Christina!

Serenity H.

The Canyon Del Oro Pirates Little League baseball team also all showed up at the funeral, and most were crying. I shared the same message with them about how we were sad but we knew Christina was in heaven.

John and I were also warmed to greet many out-of-town guests, many of them college and high school friends we had not seen in years. The nurses from the trauma team at University Medical Center were gracious and told us how emotionally affected they had been by working with our family on that terrible day.

We had expected to see a lot of people from the world of Major League Baseball, but we were stunned at how many showed up. Owners and general managers of the Dodgers, Phillies, and Diamondbacks were there, as well as about 100 scouts from around the country. John was especially touched to see Boston Red Sox player Darnell McDonald, whom he had helped sign with the Orioles years before. They had not been close over the years, but apparently Darnell had not forgotten John's contribution to his career.

Hall of Famer Ryne Sandberg, who had played with both the Phillies and the Cubs when John's dad was with both clubs, was also there.

John and I were unable to see everyone, and after ninety minutes we had to break away and head back home for a huge private reception for more than 200 family and friends.

John: We were comforted by so many people, but we were still in shock, so I don't remember many of the individual conversations. I do recall that many sat watching the funeral proceedings on TV, but Roxanna and I could not bear to watch. It was just too overwhelming emotionally.

This was the day that our friends and family had to realize what an impact our little girl had on the country, seeing all the well-wishers, the comments from the president, the huge funeral service, and all the media coverage.

One conversation I do remember was with my parents' best friends, Clyde and Lois Louth. They said that "the service, the church, and the whole atmosphere were unbelievable. That was the closest to heaven we're going to get on this earth!" Sadly, about two months later, Lois passed away unexpectedly from a brain hemorrhage. During her funeral, her husband, Clyde, referred back to Christina-Taylor's funeral as inspiration and a reminder to his family that Lois was definitely in heaven.

A lot of people asked me that day—and they still do— whether I battled anger over the death of my little girl. Well, sure, that's a temptation. When I allow myself to dwell on it, it makes no sense, it's not fair, and I don't understand a world where some erratic person can rob so many people of their loved ones.

That day, and even now, I just feel a profound sadness over the loss of such a beautiful child. I could allow myself to get angry if I wanted to, but that's not going to bring Christina-Taylor back. If I was face-to-face with the fellow that did this, yeah, you'd see some anger. But I don't want to do or say anything that makes this about him. I want everybody to see who Christina-Taylor was. I've quit worrying about him.

I try to concentrate on the positives, like all those baseball people showing up. I found out I had more friends than I ever thought. You know, pro sports is a competitive business, so even people you like as friends can be your so-called opponents on a day-to-day basis.

But we have a close-knit group in the scouting community. I hadn't seen many of them in years. A lot of them flew out to Arizona not knowing whether they'd be able to get a hotel room or even get into the church, but they showed up anyway.

Some of 'em asked why I wanted to speak in the service, meaning, of course, why did I think I could get through it? First off, I wanted to speak to Christina-Taylor. I know she was watching from heaven and that she could hear me. Then I

wanted to talk about her and let people, adults and kids, really
know who she was and that she would want us all to be okay.

Later we learned that that afternoon, the first lady had written a
letter released by the White House to parents:

Dear parents,

Like so many Americans all across the country, Barack
and I were shocked and heartbroken by the horrific act of
violence committed in Arizona this past weekend. Yester-
day, we had the chance to attend a memorial service and
meet with some of the families of those who lost their
lives, and both of us were deeply moved by their strength
and resilience in the face of such unspeakable tragedy.

As parents, an event like this hits home especially hard.
It makes our hearts ache for those who lost loved ones. It
makes us want to hug our own families a little tighter. And
it makes us think about what an event like this says about
the world we live in—and the world in which our children
will grow up.

In the days and weeks ahead, as we struggle with these
issues ourselves, many of us will find that our children are
struggling with them as well. The questions my daughters have asked are the same ones that many of your children will have—and they don't lend themselves to easy
answers. But they will provide an opportunity for us as
parents to teach some valuable lessons—about the char-

acter of our country, about the values we hold dear, and about finding hope at a time when it seems far away.

We can teach our children that here in America, we embrace each other, and support each other, in times of crisis. And we can help them do that in their own small way—whether it's by sending a letter, or saying a prayer, or just keeping the victims and their families in their thoughts.

We can teach them the value of tolerance—the practice of assuming the best, rather than the worst, about those around us. We can teach them to give others the benefit of the doubt, particularly those with whom they disagree.

We can also teach our children about the tremendous sacrifices made by the men and women who serve our country and by their families. We can explain to them that although we might not always agree with those who represent us, anyone who enters public life does so because they love their country and want to serve it.

Christina Green felt that call. She was just nine years old when she lost her life. But she was at that store that day because she was passionate about serving others. She had just been elected to her school's student council, and she wanted to meet her congresswoman and learn more about politics and public life.

And that's something else we can do for our children—we can tell them about Christina and about how much she wanted to give back. We can tell them about

John Roll, a judge with a reputation for fairness; about Dorothy Morris, a devoted wife to her husband, her high school sweetheart, to whom she'd been married for fifty-five years; about Phyllis Schneck, a great-grandmother who sewed aprons for church fundraisers; about Dorwan Stoddard, a retired construction worker who helped neighbors down on their luck; and about Gabe Zimmerman, who did community outreach for Congresswoman Giffords, working tirelessly to help folks who were struggling, and was engaged to be married next year. We can tell them about the brave men and women who risked their lives that day to save others. And we can work together to honor their legacy by following their example—by embracing our fellow citizens; by standing up for what we believe is right; and by doing our part, however we can, to serve our communities and our country.

Sincerely,

Michelle Obama

At 10:15 a.m., January 8, 2011, the first deputy on the scene detains the suspect.

CHAPTER SIXTEEN

SEEKING PEACE

LET US NOT GROW WEARY WHILE DOING GOOD, FOR IN DUE SEASON
WE SHALL REAP IF WE DO NOT LOSE HEART.
THEREFORE, AS WE HAVE OPPORTUNITY, LET US DO
GOOD TO ALL, ESPECIALLY TO THOSE WHO ARE OF THE
HOUSEHOLD OF FAITH (GALATIANS 6:9–10).

A certain sense of parental pride and even satisfaction came with having spent three straight days celebrating all the best of our precious daughter. To be surrounded and buoyed up by family and friends was a great comfort. But nothing could change the fact that we were walking wounded. Our spirits, though encouraged by sweet memories, were injured and, we feared, perhaps beyond repair. You don't get over such a loss, nor do you want to.

People were coming and going, and much as we dreaded isolation and loneliness, at times we needed to be alone. I began to wonder what I would do with myself when John went back on the road and Dallas went back to school. Part of me wondered how the world dared keep turning and life kept going on, especially the mundane day-to-day.

But John would need his work to keep his sanity. Baseball was more than what he did; it was who he was. And while there was an appropriate time for reflection, he couldn't wallow in regret and misery. He had to get back out there. And Dallas could be away from school for only so long. He needed the distraction of his studies and the support of friends.

Everything had happened so fast . . . the funeral was held not even a full week after the shootings. I knew it would take time to settle into any sort of routine, but for now I just wanted some respite, some peace in the midst of a storm of activity.

I had long been fascinated by the different ways people deal with grief. Some fall apart. Some seem unable to function at all. Others are weepy, yet others talkative. There are those who still don't understand how I was able to carry on, let alone to be able to talk about Christina-Taylor at the drop of a hat.

We were already being swamped with media requests, book and movie offers, all sorts of things. Did that seem crass? Sure it did. And we soon had to have help sorting it all out. People had to wonder how I could even think of such things at a time like that. But did they really think I didn't have my dark nights of the soul?

John and I cried until we couldn't imagine producing another tear. When one of us was at a low point, the other would be strong. At times all we could do was hold each other tight, in essence hanging on for dear life. There were moments when life didn't seem worth living. We agonized over the whys and the unfairness of it all. And all the while we kept a careful eye on Dallas.

Mostly there was a feeling of helplessness when all we could do was pray and remind ourselves that Christina-Taylor was now healthy and whole and happy in heaven. The ugliness of losing her had been thrust upon us without warning, without preparation, without our being able to do a thing about it. We hadn't even been aware she was in danger, let alone had an iota of a chance to protect her. The shock of her having been with us one instant and gone the next never seemed to soften. It struck me fresh and deep every time I thought of it.

It was as if we had been checkmated by fate before even knowing we were in a chess match. I soon got to the place where I just wanted relief, some tranquility, a place and some time to grieve my daughter with all my might.

Meanwhile, of course, I was worried about Suzi Hileman. Bill was keeping us up-to-date on her condition in the hospital, which—while not good—was thankfully not life threatening. When her ventilator was removed for the first time, Bill says her first question was, "What about Christina?" Even after he had broken the awful truth to her, Suzi would forget and sometimes cry out for Christina.

***Bill Hileman:** There was nothing to do but to tell her honestly what had happened. She knows in clear moments that she's not to blame, that it was the act of a madman. But any of us, especially parents, understand that in weaker, darker moments, you're going to go to a place that is going to haunt you for a long time.*

When her heavy meds were reduced to where she could talk about what she remembered, naturally I wanted any details she could provide. The most comforting thing I had heard so far was from the surgeon, who had assured me that the nature of Christina-Taylor's wounds indicated to him that she would hardly have had even seconds to suffer.

I knew Suzi was living with guilt, as I suppose anyone would in a similar situation. I assured her, and she had to know at some level, that no one blamed her or thought she could have done anything to change what had happened. But in her blog she wrote, "I know that it is possible to watch the light go out of another person's eyes. I do not know if it is possible to live with that knowledge. I do know that I will try."

From what I could determine, Christina-Taylor and Suzi were at the head of the line to see Congresswoman Giffords when the gunman opened fire. Everyone instinctively spun away from the sound, and most took bullets from the back, including Christina and Suzi.

"I couldn't bring her home," Suzi said. "I'm so sorry that I couldn't bring her home."

Suzi liked to reminisce about Christina-Taylor and recalled the first time they played pick-up sticks. "She cheated," Suzi says with a smile. "She would try to distract me by pointing at something across the room, and when I would look she would move the sticks. She knew that I knew exactly what she was up to, and how she would laugh!"

Suzi told me that on the way to Safeway that morning, she and Christina-Taylor talked about what they might ask the congresswoman. "And she reminded me not to lose my car keys like I often did."

Suzi also said that when Christina-Taylor was next in line and they were chatting about how many decision-makers worked in Washington, Suzi whispered to her, "You could be the next Gabrielle Giffords."

When the shots rang out and the two hit the ground, someone called out, "Who was with this girl? Who is this girl?"

Suzi says, "I said, 'She is my responsibility. She's my friend.' Of course, nine-year-old girls don't carry identification, so nobody knew who she was, except me. And now the rest of the world."

Bill Hileman: The day after her daughter passed, Roxanna herself sent a beautiful, gracious email to my wife. It was an incredible outreach.

Something else that helped me cope during that first week was another idea that originated with Leslie Crist. I had been agonizing over how to best use Christina-Taylor's legacy for something positive in the world, and Leslie said, "How about a foundation?"

From the very beginning, people were showering us with gifts of food and candy and flowers and meals. We deeply appreciated every gesture, but after a while, you run out of people to give these things to once you have used all you need. We had the feeling that Christina-Taylor—with her heart for needy people and her interest in getting involved in her community—would want to see these things used in positive ways.

We thought it was a wonderful idea, and so we established the Christina-Taylor Green Memorial Foundation as a nonprofit corporation. I know there are skeptics who will say that a nine-year-old girl wouldn't have been so altruistic, but the fact is, she was. My mother played a big part in educating her about single moms or families that don't have enough money, reminding her how blessed she was. Christina-Taylor was aware of what it's like for kids in Third World countries, so I know she would want money and resources produced by her foundation to go to people who were less fortunate and also to people who excel, get good grades, and work hard.

It was therapeutic to have something to think about, to strategize, and to create something positive from this horrible event. Over the past year—and I'm hoping for many years to come—it has kept me busy and provided a way to give back to our community.

The CTG Memorial Foundation mission is clear and simple:

It was established to galvanize projects in our community that reflect Christina-Taylor's interests, values, and dreams. These projects may include:

- Educational funding for less fortunate children and their families
- Leadership programs that promote awareness and hope to those who strive to achieve, and
- Scholastic activities throughout our community that promote a positive influence on our youth.

The Memorial Foundation evaluates grant requests that address one or more of those areas.

⁓

Our first project was a new playground at Mesa Verde Elementary, where the equipment was outdated. After hearing me on the radio talking about Christina-Taylor's legacy, the Allstate Foundation donated $150,000 for that playground. As donations kept coming in, we allocated another $50,000 to Christina-Taylor's and Dallas's school for interactive whiteboards and computers, and the same amount to Cross Middle School.

As more came in, we planned to use it for projects that reflected our daughter's interests and values. Like most states, Arizona was hit with budget cuts that affected art, music, and gym classes. This is the kind of stuff Christina loved, and of course those activities can be just as important to a kid as traditional classes.

So much money began rolling in that we had to decide how far we would look for projects to help with. Tucson had plenty of needs of its own, and it's also the community that responded so generously after the shooting; but we finally decided—as our friend, medical reporter Stephanie Innes, put it in the *Arizona Daily Star*—that our plan is to broaden our horizons. Ideally, we would like to offer scholarships to children all over Arizona and, we hope, in time raise enough money to include children from all over the United States.

"Improving playgrounds, helping teachers, getting backpacks for less fortunate kids, those are the kinds of things we'll be doing," I told Stephanie in an interview.

I couldn't forget that Christina-Taylor wanted to talk to U.S. Representative Giffords about global warming, the BP oil spill, and about what it's like to have a career in politics. In her article, Stephanie added:

> "People asked me why we didn't call this the Green Family Foundation," said Roxanna Green. "But I want this to be about Christina-Taylor. We're going to do everything in our power to make sure her legacy endures."
>
> [For the Memorial Foundation] Green has designed pink and black pins in the shape of a baseball that say CTG on them. The foundation will sell them as fundraisers, along with Christina-Taylor Green patches and bracelets.
>
> "Christina-Taylor was amazingly happy all the time," Green said. "If she ever felt a little down, she'd snap out of it, and I know I have to do that too. It helps me heal to give back, and doing it in my daughter's name gives me a lot of joy and pleasure."

About a week after the shooting, Jan Booth, a mutual friend and neighbor of Suzi Hileman, came to visit me and said she had Christina-Taylor's hoodie from Suzi's car, the one I had made her run back in the house for that fateful morning. Jan asked if it would be okay for her to bring it to me on her next visit. I was thrilled. What a priceless gift.

Everything else had been confiscated by the FBI and the police, so here was a piece of clothing she hadn't worn that day, but that she'd had with her. I gave Jan a huge hug when I tearfully thanked her, and I still keep that hoodie near my bed.

The Hoffmans, who owned the karate school where Dallas trained, had attended Christina-Taylor's memorial services. I wrote them a long card of thanks and took it to them when Dallas went back to class later in January. It was so good to be able to embrace them and tell them how blessed and grateful I was for that class. John told Mr. Hoffman that had it not been for karate that Saturday morning, Dallas would probably have gone with Christina-Taylor and perhaps lost his life as well.

Also later in January we received a wonderful letter from Roger L. Williams, executive director of the Penn State Alumni Association. His letter expressed their condolences and said, "All of us were shocked and saddened by this heinous act. At the same time, we were greatly inspired by all Christina had accomplished in her young life and her goals, which, as news reports stated, included attending Penn State . . .

" . . . the Penn State Alumni Association will memorialize Christina's dream with the installation of a 'bluestone' on Alumni Walk, a brick-and-stone sidewalk outside the University's Hintz Family Alumni Center with the names of more than four thousand Alumni Association members.

" . . . The inscription reads: In Memory of Christina Green / Her Dream Was Penn State.

"I hope this will convey the esteem in which we hold Christina's life and memory. We will forever consider her a true Penn Stater."

It might be hard to imagine someone even considering turning down an invitation to Washington for the State of the Union address, which was scheduled for January 25, 2011. We were so honored to be asked, and the president and first lady had been so kind to us just five days after the shooting. But John and I really had to talk it through.

We almost declined. We're talking just seventeen days after the loss of our child, and we had been so busy we'd hardly had time to think and reflect. The thought of traveling across the country, staying in a hotel—well, it sounded like an ordeal.

We needed time and space to mourn alone, and yet we also knew that if we went, we would feel uniquely close to Christina-Taylor because of her interest in government. You can bet this is a trip she never would have passed up. We finally came to the conclusion that for the sake of the kids—both Christina and Dallas—we needed to do it. She had been such a fan of the president, had naively but sweetly wanted to invite them to join us for a ballgame in Washington the year before, and had been trying to educate herself politically the day she died. And for Dallas, this could be a once-in-a-lifetime opportunity.

Under almost any other circumstances, it would have been fun to dress up for a pre-speech reception at the White House and to enjoy the architecture, the history, the chandeliers, piano music, being waited on, and getting one-on-one time with Michelle Obama. It was a privilege, but naturally it was bittersweet and melancholy for us.

Dallas finally got to meet the First Dog, Bo, which he enjoyed. And the first lady urged him to skip the State of the Union speech. She told him that people would be standing to applaud and sitting down, then standing and sitting again all evening, and that it was even too much for a couple of veterans like her daughters. "You can play with the girls and the dog if you'd rather . . . "

At first I thought Dallas was declining out of shyness, but he was clear. "No, I want to go. I know this is important, and I want to be there."

After enjoying *hors d'oeuvres* and a nice dinner, we were loaded into vans to be transported to the House of Representatives chamber of the Capitol building where the president would address a joint session of the U.S. Congress.

The pomp and circumstance was impressive, and this was the State of the Union address where the members of Congress were urged to not sit by party but rather intermingle.

President Obama began his remarks that night:

> Mr. Speaker, Mr. Vice President, members of Congress, distinguished guests, and fellow Americans:
>
> Tonight I want to begin by congratulating the men and women of the 112th Congress, as well as your new Speaker, John Boehner. And as we mark this occasion, we're also mindful of the empty chair in this chamber, and we pray for the health of our colleague—and our friend—Gabby Giffords.
>
> It's no secret that those of us here tonight have had our differences over the last two years. The debates have been contentious; we have fought fiercely for our beliefs. And that's a good thing. That's what a robust democracy demands. That's what helps set us apart as a nation.
>
> But there's a reason the tragedy in Tucson gave us pause. Amid all the noise and passion and rancor of our public debate, Tucson reminded us that no matter who we are or where we come from, each of us is a part of

something greater—something more consequential than party or political preference.

We are part of the American family. We believe that in a country where every race and faith and point of view can be found, we are still bound together as one people; that we share common hopes and a common creed; that the dreams of a little girl in Tucson are not so different than those of our own children, and that they all deserve the chance to be fulfilled.

That, too, is what sets us apart as a nation . . . [1]

⟳

Hours later we got to shake hands with the president once again and to have our pictures taken with him. Finally it was back to our hotel and then flying home the next day. That distinguished event capped a month unlike any we had ever experienced or wished to experience ever again.

While I was determined to keep working passionately on the Christina-Taylor Green Memorial Foundation and make the absolute best of a devastating turn of events, you can imagine how bleak the future looked to me right then.

Medical personnel begin to arrive at 10:19 a.m., Saturday, January 8, 2011. Engines and rescue units from the Northwest Fire District begin to treat victims.

CHAPTER SEVENTEEN

THE VISITATION

LET YOUR LIGHT SO SHINE BEFORE MEN, THAT THEY MAY SEE YOUR
GOOD WORKS AND GLORIFY YOUR FATHER
IN HEAVEN (MATTHEW 5:16).

In late January and then in early February, I had two visits that meant the world to me—one from the FBI and one from God.

The FBI had been kindly keeping us up-to-date on the investigation, and as helpful as that had been, it merely caused us to keep reliving something we never wanted to think about again. It also put emphasis on the perpetrator, someone we had decided not to allow to have one more iota of influence on our lives.

He had already robbed us of a priceless treasure, and to allow our minds to dwell on him another second would only allow him to rob us of any bit of peace we could find.

But a visit from the FBI soon after we got back from Washington strangely brought with it a sweet memento that I will always cherish. They had no more need for Christina-Taylor's sapphire earrings and returned them to me. At certain times my daughter seems closer to me than others, and this was one of those times when I really felt her presence. How precious to have those reminders!

Then, about a month later, God sent me a gift I will never forget. It should come as no surprise that February had been a brutal month. The whirlwind of January had only slightly buffered the ache of loss. We had been so busy and so public with our grief that we longed for alone time. Whatever distraction there was in all the activity—and whatever worth that held—had worn off, and my times of solitude were often cruelly cold.

We are people of faith. I am a woman of prayer. I was through with the *whys* and especially the *why me's*. I just wanted some relief from a pain, an agony, so deep I couldn't imagine an end to it. Part of me didn't want it to ever really end, and it won't. But the piercing, throbbing nature of it was killing me. I felt like a boxer who had been dealt a blow that had me on the canvas. I could hear the referee's count, and it was at nine.

John was suffering too, of course, and I knew the danger that shared grief could bring to a marriage. In our case it drew us closer, and we couldn't imagine trying to endure a second of this without each other. But there were times when he was in tears and in such obvious pain that I didn't know what I had to offer him. All I could do was touch him, hold him, as he did for me when I was the one deep in the pit of despair.

Often we talked late into the night, remembering, rehashing good times, trying to find things that would allow us a sad smile or chuckle. There were many such stories and anecdotes, but too often the brief respite from mourning was quickly replaced by the reminder that we would never again build such memories of Christina-Taylor. All we had was what we could remember of nine wonderful years.

A little more than a month after the tragedy, John and I lay in bed late into the night, talking, remembering, crying. At long last, we drifted off. Some nights one of us would sleep soundly, finally surrendering to the deep fatigue long-term grief brings, while the other would toss and turn, unable to turn off the theater of the mind.

Lately I had been agonizing over Christina-Taylor's last seconds. I knew it was futile to worry about them, but I so wanted to believe that the surgeon knew best and had not just been trying to make me feel better when he told me she could not have suffered long and likely would have been gone before she hit the ground. I didn't want to think about her crying out for me, needing me. And yet it was hard to think of anything else.

Suzi Hileman's memory of Christina-Taylor's last moment seemed contrary to a merciful, instant death. But even if she remembered looking into Christina's beautiful eyes and pleading with her to stay alive, that didn't mean Christina had still been with us.

Bottom line, I missed my daughter, I ached for her, longed to hold her, and couldn't shake the haunting feeling that she might have been terrified and needed me.

This night was my turn to sleep deeply. I don't recall tossing or turning. I had tried to keep myself busy that week and that day with activities for the foundation and keeping track of Dallas's schedule. And now I was out.

At about three o'clock in the morning I felt as if I were jolted awake, though I know it was a dream. Suddenly before my eyes was the brightest, whitest light I had ever seen, and as it came into focus, it was Christina-Taylor's face with a huge smile.

I held my breath, just gazing at her beauty and wanting this— whatever it was—never to stop. She said, "Hi, Mommy. I'm in heaven with Grandma. Don't worry about me anymore, and don't be sad, because I'm really, really happy. I like it here. It's a wonderful place."

And with that, the vision, the visitation, was gone. I wanted to immediately fall back to sleep and regain it, but I couldn't. I looked at the clock. Three a.m. I wanted to tell John, but he was sound asleep and I didn't want to interrupt his much-needed rest.

When we both got up that morning, I told him, and I could tell from how he looked at me that I still had a glow from what I had experienced. And of course it thrilled him too. There's no question it was a dream, but it was also real. I believe God allowed her to communicate with me. While I still have my deep, deep lows, I look back on that experience in the wee hours of a February morning and I know Christina-Taylor is happy and in heaven.

⌒⌒

I felt bad for John's dad later that month when early in spring training down in Florida, he finally had to talk to the press about his loss. He was quoted, "I'm supposed to be a tough sucker, but I'm not tough when it comes to this."

In about twenty minutes of talking to reporters he apologized for not getting back to everyone and returning calls. He spoke about Christina-Taylor, whom he called his Princess.

"She embodied what's good about kids, and what's good about growing up in the United States. She loved doing what she did. Her interest in politics and going to that function, being in the wrong place at the wrong time, hit an awful lot of people hard. She was a wonderful little gal. We miss her desperately.

"Even though I'm a hunter and I love to have my guns, I don't have a Glock with a magazine with thirty-three bullets in it. It doesn't make sense to sell those kinds of things. I guess I never thought about it until this happened, but what reason is there to have those kinds of guns other than to kill people? I just don't understand that."

⁓

The Arizona Diamondbacks and the Chicago White Sox played a charity game at Kino Veterans Memorial Park in Tucson with proceeds pledged to the Christina-Taylor Green Memorial Foundation. John was thrilled and said, "Our family has been overwhelmed by the outpouring of love for our sweet Christina. This charitable fund will ensure her legacy for the children in our community."

The green outfield wall, which is usually covered with advertisements, carried only Christina-Taylor's jersey for that game. Normally, being out in public all the time for memorial events was tough because it caused us to relive the tragedy. People are always so wonderful, even strangers offering their sympathy. But this game was bittersweet because she so loved baseball.

Many have asked what gets us through this tragedy, and I answer, "What's getting us through is our faith."

"We understand she's in heaven," John said. "With her being born on 9/11 and the message she was able to get across to the rest of the country, I think she's in good hands."

Dallas enjoyed getting to throw out the first pitch.

John told people that the game was something Christina-Taylor would have been very proud of, and I said I wanted them to remember her as "a giver, someone always looking out for people less fortunate."

Nearly 7,500 people showed up for the game, and it was estimated that it would raise between thirty and fifty-thousand dollars for the Memorial Foundation. Imagine how pleased we were a few days later to be presented a check for nearly seventy-one thousand dollars by the Pima County Board of Supervisors.

John said, "We'd like to thank the thousands of Tucsonans who came to Kino Stadium to remember Christina-Taylor and to celebrate her life and help our community build a better future."

Tucson supported and embraced us during a rough time, and we remain determined to give back in a way Christina-Taylor would want.

"Our daughter would've been proud of our community," John said. "What Christina would want, what she would stand for, and whatever need is out there, that's what we are going to respond to."

⸻

Over the next several weeks and months God began sending me more people and things that helped give me comfort.

The first came from a stranger, as did so many gifts. People we had never heard of sent us things from all over. It was sweet and encouraging. A woman sent Dallas a book called *Heaven Is for Real: A Little Boy's Astounding Story of His Trip to Heaven and Back* by Todd Burpo with Lynn Vincent. Being a typical mother, I wasn't about to let Dallas read a book I hadn't checked out, so I read it first. Was I glad I did! This little boy's experience sounded just like what I had heard from Christina-Taylor in the middle of the night.

Yet another gift from God came not long after, when two different people told me I needed to talk to a Nancy Bowman. She had called Mesa Verde Elementary with an account of the shooting that was a little different than what other people were saying, and the assistant principal emailed me and suggested I call her when I was up to it. I wasn't yet.

And then Dallas's teacher, who was volunteering at our house one day, also urged me to talked to Nancy Bowman. Still I put it off, even though they told me that she was a nurse and her husband was a doctor and that they had been grocery shopping at the Safeway when the shooting happened.

I admit I was afraid to call her at first because I didn't know what I'd hear. I was trying to deal with what I already knew and I wasn't ready to sign up for more heartache. Then we got so busy and there didn't seem enough hours in the day, so I put off calling her. Finally one weekend I just called, and I'm glad I did.

Nancy sounded motherly and professional, and she explained how she and her husband had run from the store and immediately started tending to the victims. Her husband set up instant triage, trying to determine pulse, breathing, and severity of injuries. One thing Mrs. Bowman was sure of was that just an instant after they had heard the shots, she saw Christina-Taylor and knew she was gone.

"Your daughter looked pristine," she said, "perfect, beautiful, lying there peacefully. Experience tells me when someone has passed, and she had." She told me she had heard—as I had—lots of stories about conversations at the end. Nancy chose her words carefully but said that any conversation would have been one-sided, "because your daughter was already in heaven."

I can't tell you what a comfort it was to hear that from a professional. And she was so kind. It was a huge gift.

Something else I learned from Nancy was that it was she who talked to Bill Hileman that day. Suzi had dialed him after she and Christina-Taylor had been shot, but Nancy took the phone. She says she didn't want to alarm him more than necessary, so she just said there'd been an accident and that Suzi and Christina-Taylor would be delivered to UMC.

Then a friend told me he had heard from a woman police officer who was also immediately on the scene and wanted to talk with me about having been assigned to Christina-Taylor on the scene. When I called her, it was so good to hear from her too that Christina was clearly gone as soon as she saw her. "Mother to mother," she said, "I knew you'd want to know that."

The news media was consistent in saying that of the six people who died, five died at the scene and that the youngest, the nine-year-old girl, had died at the hospital. I remain convinced that this came from so many professionals refusing to give up on her. But I have no lingering doubts about her suffering longer than an instant.

Meanwhile, John was having his own little encouraging moments.

John: One of my biggest fears had been starting my traveling up again and getting back out onto the road, because I was still reliving this every day. One of the first things I had to come to grips with was that a lot of people felt strange even talking to me. As I've said, pro baseball is a small fraternity. Just about everybody knows everybody and you'd have had to have been living under a rock to not know that a Dodger scout and a Phillies executive had lost a member of their family.

Every year we renew our friendships in different ballparks in North Carolina, Georgia, Florida, southern California, you name it, all across the country. All of a sudden I'm seeing people I haven't seen for months, and certainly not since the shooting. Some old friends and acquaintances would come up and wrap their arms around me, and others—just as close in the past— were hesitant. More than once I found someone looking sadly at me, and I'd say, "It's okay. It's hard, but we're doing all right."

I realized that everybody needed to have that pressure-relieving conversation before we could just pick up and start talking baseball like we always had before. You couldn't just pretend your friend hadn't been through the worst of traumas.

It was clear that everybody knew what had happened, and it seemed they were all humbled by it. Most of the guys are fathers, so they can understand the awful pain. They saw our family on TV, with the president, and a lot of 'em told me how proud they were of the way we handled everything. Well, we were just hanging on the best we could, but them saying that made me proud to be a member of the baseball community, and I felt like they were glad we were part of it too.

I was at a Georgia Tech game scouting a pitcher one of the first weekends I was out. People were very kind to me and saying nice things, but it was too soon and I was really suffering.

During a break between innings, when they play music over the loudspeakers, one of Christina-Taylor's favorite songs came on and I just about lost it. I was supposed to be a professional doing my job, so I didn't want to break down in public, but I was really tearing up. I was praying, "Lord, just help me be strong."

Then a fan stands up and I notice his shirt. It reads: "Out of tragedy and chaos comes hope."

I believe God sent me that little message that day. I sure needed it. I sat there thinking, That's how we feel. People continually ask how we got through this, and I don't really know, outside of our faith. But it's important to us that the message goes beyond her being the little girl that was killed. We want people to know who she was, what she stood for.

Jamie Stone, one of Christina-Taylor's best girlfriends, had lots of play dates with her. They had hiked Sabino Canyon together, and they had both been very active in Kids Helping Kids at Mesa Verde Elementary. I remember them being involved in food, clothing, and toy drives, treating orphaned children to pizza and ice cream parties at group homes, and making gift baskets for the holidays.

Christina-Taylor's passing was very hard for Jamie, so it was special when she got to be involved in a wonderful evening of tribute to Christina in March of 2011. A local artist had fashioned a four-foot, fifty-five-pound rustic wrought iron statue of an angel in Christina's honor, and Jamie's family offered the use of their truck for us to get it home. She and her mother, Paige, and her brother Jeremy came to pick up Dallas and me, and we all went to visit the artist's studio.

Other local artists were having an open house for the public and were serving fancy snacks and refreshments on a beautiful, moon-lit night. When we brought the statue home and set it in our front yard, we all agreed that it was Christina-Taylor's kind of night and event and that it seemed she was right there with us.

A couple of months later the same family helped Dallas and me plant a flower garden around the statue. Jamie picked out the flowers and her mom bought them. Jamie said she chose red, white, and blue flowers, because that is what Christina-Taylor would have wanted.

The next week some children brought colorful pinwheels they had made, and we placed those in the new garden. We now refer to the garden as Christina-Taylor's quiet place.

Jamie later wrote a letter to Christina and gave it to me.

Dear Christina,

The night we went to pick up the angel, the moon was as bright and patriotic as you always were. I know I am very fortunate to have known you.

A playground is going to be built and dedicated in your honor, and when everyone plays there, we will know you are right there playing with us. We are getting a shade over the entire thing and rubbery ground all around for safety. Whenever I look up at the sky I know you are looking right back at me. I miss you.

Here's a poem I wrote for you:

When I look up at the sky, I know the brightest star is you.

The night we brought the angel home, I knew you were smiling too.

Your story will live forever, and it has taught me to never say never.

Even a decade later, you'll still be in our hearts forever.

Your friend,

Jamie Stone

⌒

Late in February we were honored when Canada Del Oro Linear Park, just five minutes from our home, was renamed Christina-Taylor Green Memorial Linear Park. The St. Odilia Children's Choir that Christina had sung in, Joyful Noise, sang "God Bless America," "America the Beautiful," and "This Land Is Your Land." Pink and purple balloons were released with messages inside to inspire kids to greatness and to make a difference.

One of the most special tributes to Christina-Taylor came in April when the town of Oro Valley dedicated a much bigger statue—Freedom's Steadfast Angel of Love—in her honor at the Canyon Del Oro Little League Field Number One that was also named Green Field after her.

There was already a tribute to Christina-Taylor on the CDO Little League website, written by her coach, John Ward, and it had been there since a couple of days after the shooting. It read, in part:

The tragedy on Saturday has taken one of our own, Christina-Taylor Green, a Little Leaguer in every sense of the title.

Christina played baseball in the Canyon Del Oro Little League for the Fall Pirates in 2009 and 2010. Her dad, John, was a valued coach and friend on both teams, while sharing his dedication and talents with his son Dallas's team at the same time.

Christina's story should be shared, both as a possible aid in the healing process for the family and community, but also as a source of inspiration to all of us.

Christina's love for the game of baseball did not have to be learned or developed. The family connections to the game made it a part of who she was. What she exemplified in the baseball arena were the core characteristics we all hope our players will gain from Little League baseball: Character, Courage, and Loyalty.

CHARACTER: A sense of right and wrong, a willingness to do something about wrongs, a desire to learn, a determination to excel, and a fun-loving attitude. We've all heard of Christina's ability to demonstrate these attributes on the baseball field.

She was competitive. She wanted to excel, and she also wanted her team to excel. But she understood that there was more to Little League than just winning or losing. She was as upset as anyone when a bad play occurred, but she was also as excited as anyone after a good play.

One particular memory involves Christina flipping the ball from her second base position to the shortstop covering second. The base runner made a clean but hard slide to break up the play, and a bit of a scuffle started. Christina, the only girl on the field, immediately took charge and set the players straight. Her attitude and actions exuded the Character of a leader.

COURAGE: Christina was not short on Courage. She played with boys who were strong and fast, but she never once was fazed about being the only girl on the team, nor did a hard-hit ball or a whizzing fastball intimidate her.

In one game, Christina was fouling several balls off, and after six or seven pitches, a fastball plunked her pretty good. She was given the choice to take first base or finish her at bat (instructional league rules). With a slight grimace but without hesitation, she said, "I want to hit." And hit she did! She drove a hard hit on the next pitch. Courage was part of who she was.

LOYALTY: When a child demonstrates loyalty without prompting, we know it comes from them and not just from parental prodding. Christina was one who would always reach out to a teammate in need of a "nice try" or "get 'em next time." When cheering was needed from the dugout, she could be counted on to get it started.

But her loyalty to her team can best be demonstrated by the fact that a message was received early one Saturday morning from her dad, John, that Christina was under the weather and wasn't going to make it to the game. During warm-ups before the game, we were shocked to see her show up. You could tell she didn't feel too hot, but

Dad explained, "She wanted to play ball, to be here for the team." That was Christina's Loyalty.

Christina was a great second baseman, an up-and-coming pitcher, a strong batter, and an outstanding teammate. May we all accept the challenge to glorify Christina by finding our own little ways to live life to the fullest, to demonstrate CHARACTER, COURAGE, and LOYALTY with the zest Christina did.

⁓

The statue of the angel was unveiled at the start of the spring season before a five o'clock game on April 1, 2011, at James D. Kriegh Park. Significantly, it stood nine feet eleven inches and the artist, Lei Hennessy-Owen—who traveled from Pennsylvania to finish assembling it on site—included two boulders from the Flight 93 crash site and wreckage from the World Trade Center and the Pentagon.

That the angel was made from the remnants of the 9/11 attacks made it especially touching. Christina-Taylor had always wanted to be a symbol of hope for those touched by that great tragedy the day she was born.

Hundreds of people showed up to celebrate with us and to dedicate the newly named baseball field. The program included the Canyon Del Oro High School choir, a color guard, two bagpipers, a speech by the Mayor of Oro Valley, remarks from Dodger assistant general manager Logan White, and John, who said, "I can see her big smile up in heaven right now. All of us should do everything we can to make sure this country lives up to our children's expectations. Christina shows us how to come together as a community and care for one another."

We were presented with a framed sixty-pound stainless-steel replica of Christina-Taylor's Little League jersey. Dallas got to throw the ceremonial first pitch.

It was also announced that a special patch bearing Christina's initials would be worn on the CDO Little League uniforms to remember Christina-Taylor. It had her initials on a baseball, the American flag, and the twin towers of the World Trade Center in the background.

The April 1 event was really special and a tribute that will stay with us for the rest of our lives. It was moving and touching. We had goose bumps. We were proud and honored and pleased.

⁓

John and I were touched later in the month when we got a note from the Indianapolis Colts' star quarterback.

> Dear Mr. and Mrs. Green,
>
> I am very sorry for your loss. Please know that you and your family are in Ashley's and my thoughts and prayers. I saw a special on TV on Christina last week. I can tell she was a special girl and that she will be missed by many. All my best to you both.
>
> Sincerely,
>
> Peyton Manning
>
> *Matthew 4:5: "Blessed are those who mourn, for they will be comforted."*[1]

Ten ground ambulances and three air ambulances arrive at 10:24 a.m., Saturday, January 8, 2011. The wounded are removed within forty minutes. Six patients die, including a nine-year-old girl.

CHAPTER EIGHTEEN

ENDURING

Love your enemies, bless those who curse you,
do good to those who hate you,
and pray for those who spitefully use you and persecute you,
that you may be sons of your Father in
heaven (Matthew 5:44–45a).

Our first Easter without Christina-Taylor started very rough for me. The resurrection of Jesus Christ is central to our faith, and all my life I had enjoyed dressing up to celebrate it. Growing up, it had never been about new spring clothes or some Easter parade. And neither were we people who attended church only on Easter and Christmas. This was our life. Imagine my joy over the years to dress Christina-Taylor appropriately for Easter, and then as she grew older to see her share in the excitement and help choose her own outfits.

Fortunately for me, come Easter Sunday, April 24, 2011, we had very special houseguests with us for a week. Michele Wimer and her daughter Kendall had flown in from Conowingo, Maryland, and it's hard to explain how much that meant to me, just three and a half months after losing Christina-Taylor. Michele had been one of the first friends I had made when we moved to the farm so many years before, and we have been close ever since.

Back in the days when Dallas was having so much trouble and John wasn't totally up to speed with all that yet, Michele and her husband, Don, really helped me out. Their older daughter, Alexis, would babysit for me, and later she would even stay overnight with me in Pennsylvania when John was away on long trips.

Frankly, I can't imagine life over the years without Michele. I consider her the older sister I never had, a devout Christian lady who became a mentor and special friend. My kids called her Aunt Michele, and her kids called me Aunt Roxanna.

So, in my deep pain and grief, I felt blessed to have Michele there on such a melancholy day. The five of us went to church together, but because it was so crowded, we were unable to sit in our favorite spot. That wasn't a big deal but just added to my discomfort. Seeing other little girls all dressed up would normally interest and delight me, but now it just broke my heart. I was there with my family and two close friends, but Christina-Taylor's absence left such a void.

I was so emotional that it was all I could do to keep it together as we sat down. Nothing was said, but I knew John and Dallas were filled with thoughts of our daughter and sister.

With a few minutes to go before the service started, John reached in the pew rack for a prayer book, and as he opened it a handmade bookmark slipped and fluttered to the floor. When he picked it up and quietly showed it to me, it was obvious it had been drawn on by a child. There was a little girl smiling, with flowers blooming, birds flying, and a bright, smiling sun. The artwork and style was similar to what Christina-Taylor liked to do.

I knew it was not hers, but I believe God put that there for John to find and to comfort us—to remind us that she was fine, she was happy, and she was there with us in spirit that day. John slipped it into his coat pocket and it remains a treasure.

The next month the Christina-Taylor Green Memorial Foundation announced a cooperative with Running Start, a nonprofit group dedicated to educating young women about politics. We established a scholarship to allow Southern Arizona girls to participate in a Political Leadership Program.

Their scholarships had been typically for high school girls, but the Christina-Taylor Green Memorial Scholarship would extend the age down to nine-year-olds, in Christina's honor.

Emma McMahon was awarded our first Running Start scholarship. Her mother, Mary, had been shot several times shielding Emma during the January 8 attack.

John was quoted, "Our family has been overwhelmed by the outpouring of love for our sweet Christina. This scholarship is another way to ensure her legacy for the children in our community."

At the end of the elementary school year in late May, we added to the playground and computer gifts from the fund to Mesa Verde by hosting a luncheon for the faculty, employees, and staff. We were determined that it be more than just sandwiches. We provided a nice hot meal for everyone as an encouragement and thank you.

At around that same time, we were given an award by the Eye Bank Association of America for the donation of Christina-Taylor's corneas. We had heard, of course, that this had given someone else sight, and we knew Christina would be thrilled and proud.

Such honors are humbling and in their own way help take the sharp edges off the pain that still assaults us every day. Would I rather have my daughter back? Of course I would. But I'm so grateful that, short of that, part of her lives on to help others.

———

John continued to suffer in his own silent way but found it therapeutic while alone on the road to write out his thoughts. Twice this came out in simple poetry, not something he was accustomed to writing; but it spoke deeply to me and to anyone else who saw it.

"Faith"
    Christina-Taylor Green on one-eight-eleven
    Was laid to rest and went to heaven.

    She left her mark in nine short years,
    And we remain to shed our tears.

    Mom, Dad, and Dallas will love you forever,
    Awaiting the day we're again together.

"Inspiration"

> Out of tragedy and chaos came your hopes and dreams
> Nine-eleven was not enough, it seems.
>
> Your big brown eyes and angelic smile
> Made the world a better place, at least for a while.
>
> God's plan will keep you busy, we know;
> It goes without saying, we miss you so.
>
> Wish I could tell you I love you and you'll be all right.
> God needed you more; we didn't win that fight.
>
> Your family will miss you, your friends and country too.
> You're an inspiration, we're so proud of you.

Both John and I continued to monitor Dallas and his reaction to all of this. Boys at that age can be hard to read anyway, but coming up on his twelfth birthday, he had already had his share of challenges in life, even before losing his sister and best friend.

We didn't want to be naive about it, but it seemed he was doing remarkably well. He often shared memories of his sister, whatever popped into his head at the moment. He talked as if she was right there with us and had a peace about him that seemed to say he knew she was okay in heaven. He even talked to his friends and shared stories about her, and I think this put them at ease, because many people don't know what to say or how to bring up the subject.

Naturally certain memories made him sad, like when he went to her room or saw pictures of her, and he shed tears like we did.

But he also very much enjoyed talking about Christina-Taylor and would volunteer memories that were sparked by things he saw, places we went, people we talked to.

Recently he wrote out three of his favorite memories of Christina-Taylor:

Food Fight

When I was almost four and Christina-Taylor almost two, I think Mom thought we were both taking naps. She didn't know we were in the kitchen and that I had discovered two cartons of eggs in the refrigerator. What could be more fun that that?

I gave Christina one of the cartons and opened it for her and said, "Let's see how many times you can hit me with these eggs." She started throwing them at me. Then I threw one that hit her right in the face, but instead of crying she laughed. When she ran out of eggs and I had two left, I held one over her and dropped it on her head. That's about the time Mom heard us and came running. When she saw what we had done to the kitchen, we got into trouble.

That Christmas we did the same thing with some Christmas balls, throwing them against the wall. Christina ran away from the loud noise of them breaking, and I cut myself on one of them.

Christina's First Hair Salon

When Christina-Taylor was four and I was six, we lived in West Grove, Pennsylvania, and she started a hair salon in the basement. Her first customer was a girl from next door. That girl's brother—my friend—and I came downstairs from watching TV and saw what she did to this poor girl's hair.

The girl did not have a mirror and thought her hair looked nice, but there was hair all over the floor and what was left on her head looked really bad. Christina-Taylor was proud of her work and both girls seemed very happy, so Christina gave herself a trim as well. Remember, no mirror.

She offered to cut my hair too, but I refused because I knew what was coming. When our mother and the girl's mother saw them, we could hear the screaming and ran to see what was going on. Christina-Taylor was so busted.

Cape Cod

Christina-Taylor and I always looked forward to going to the Cape Cod beaches because we always had so much fun swimming. Eating crab reminded me of the time we were hunting for hermit crabs and found a giant live sand crab.

Suddenly it jumped on Christina's foot and she started screaming and was bleeding a little. When I went to get it off her, it leaped from her foot to my head and got tangled in my hair. Dad finally came over and put a bandage on Christina's foot while I worked to get that crab out of my hair. I threw it onto the beach where it was attacked and eaten by sea gulls.

We caught a lot of hermit crabs that day, so we still had fun.

⁓

It was also heartwarming to get notes and messages and memories from people in Christina-Taylor's life. I especially appreciated getting the following from one of her early teachers:

Green Family—

Christina was in my first grade class, but she has never stopped being a "Tucker." Last year she would come to my class to give Kids Helping Kids announcements. Most of the time she would come just to say hi to the students and to see what unit we were working on and tell them what she remembered about the subject. She was always welcome, and the kids loved it when she would come in and share. Often she would come over just to give me a big hug and give me an update on herself or her class or family. The last time I got to get one of her monster hugs was the day before Christmas break, 2010. She and her best friend Serenity came to wish me a Merry Christmas, and Christina gave me a present of hot chocolate. I cherish that I had that opportunity . . . .

This special story Christina had me share with her several times. She was so proud of her family and spoke of you all often. The first time I met her daddy was at the first grade parent meet/greet. This mountain of a man walked in with this deep voice, and I was shaking with fear (Christina thought that part was hilarious). Her dad said, "Christina's mother told me I needed to bring healthy snacks for the class, but I couldn't help myself when I saw these." He handed me a bag that had healthy snacks, but on top were a couple packages of Double Stuf Oreos! I knew then that this was going to be a fun family. Christina thought her daddy was the coolest thing.

She was just a bundle of sunshine and would scatter her joy everywhere she went. She told me often that she wanted to be a vet or to help people. What she shared most were happy things about her family, who meant everything to her. Honestly, you were heroes to her.

Thank you for sharing that precious baby with me. She is still a "Tucker."
Many Blessings,
Sarah Tucker
1st Grade Teacher
Mesa Verde Elementary

We were honored beyond words at Major League Baseball's annual All-Star game in July 2011. Just six months since losing Christina-Taylor, John and Dallas and I were asked to ceremoniously bring out the lineup cards before the game. It was great to meet the managers and shake hands with all the umpires.

The game was held at the Arizona Diamondbacks' Chase Field in Phoenix, which made it handy for us, and of course John would have gone anyway as part of his job. It was the perfect place to honor the victims, and because of Christina-Taylor's relationship to John and Grandpa Dallas Green, baseball considered her part of the family.

"She definitely would have been here," John told the press. "This is definitely right down her alley. It was very emotional, but it was a fitting place to honor our daughter and the other families who lost people in the Tucson tragedy. The baseball community got behind us. We always felt that, but it showed the other families how good the baseball industry is at taking care of people. We appreciate it. It meant a lot to us for our son to be here. Christina would have loved to have been here. We still miss her unbelievably. One thing we don't want is for people to forget."

The All-Star managers, Bruce Bochy and Ron Washington, were nice to Dallas, and we were surprised to see one of the players, Andre Ethier, still wearing a purple Christina bracelet from our Foundation that all the Dodgers had worn at a charity game in Tucson. John didn't know he'd still be wearing it, but Andre is an Arizonan and a Dodger, so he knows what we were going through. He told us that he never takes it off.

Bochy, manager of the San Francisco Giants, said the lineup-card ceremony was "pretty emotional. It breaks your heart what happened. She was a beautiful young girl, and for her family to go through that . . . The players were talking about it, so it was nice to have the Greens out here. It was a special moment, I thought, but a very tough moment for us and for the family."

⁓

Little League Baseball also honored Christina-Taylor by inviting us to meet with the family of firefighter Michael Cammarata at the

65th Little League Baseball World Series in Williamsport, Penn-sylvania, on Saturday, August 27.

Michael died at the World Trade Center the day Christina was born, and both had been Little League players. The organization unveiled a huge replica on the outfield fence of a patch the teams wore for the tournament. It read MC/CTG.

Dallas got the honor of throwing the ceremonial first pitch, and it didn't surprise me that it was a perfect strike.

At 8:20 p.m., Saturday, January 8, 2011, a dozen police cars remain at the scene, surrounding the Safeway. The store would not reopen for a week.

CHAPTER NINETEEN

LEGACY OF A PRINCESS

IN ALL THINGS WE COMMEND OURSELVES AS MINISTERS OF GOD:
IN MUCH PATIENCE, IN TRIBULATIONS, IN NEEDS, IN DISTRESSES,
IN STRIPES, IN IMPRISONMENTS, IN TUMULTS, IN LABORS, IN
SLEEPLESSNESS, IN FASTINGS; BY PURITY, BY KNOWLEDGE, BY
LONGSUFFERING, BY KINDNESS, BY THE HOLY SPIRIT, BY SINCERE
LOVE, BY THE WORD OF TRUTH, BY THE POWER OF GOD, BY THE
ARMOR OF RIGHTEOUSNESS ON THE RIGHT HAND AND ON THE
LEFT, BY HONOR AND DISHONOR, BY EVIL REPORT AND GOOD
REPORT; AS DECEIVERS, AND YET TRUE; AS UNKNOWN, AND YET
WELL KNOWN; AS DYING, AND BEHOLD WE LIVE; AS CHASTENED,
AND YET NOT KILLED; AS SORROWFUL, YET ALWAYS REJOICING;
AS POOR, YET MAKING MANY RICH; AS HAVING NOTHING, AND
YET POSSESSING ALL THINGS (2 CORINTHIANS 6:4–10).

As the work of the Christina-Taylor Green Memorial Foundation continued and honors and tributes and letters kept pouring in, our lives grew only busier. Some might assume that this helped assuage our grief. Time does heal, to a degree, but only to a degree.

It's helpful to be busy, and it's gratifying to see Christina's spirit and legacy carried on. I love knowing that people are being blessed by the brief life she lived and what has come since her death.

When I look back at the footage of the events we attended and the things we did the very week following her death, I can see I was just forcing myself to go through the motions. It was all I could do to get through each day, exhausted, going without sleep, and with hardly a minute to myself to just suffer alone. The phone never stopped ringing; the mail never slowed. We had to get a P. O. box in town because there was too much mail to deliver to the house. We had to have help just going through all the letters. And all while reeling from a dreadful blow.

We received rosaries, handmade crocheted angels, quilts, blankets, photos, paintings, things from school classes, trinkets and mementos of all kinds, plus letters and cards. We thought it would be too much for Dallas, so after he was asleep we would take Rubbermaid boxes full of stuff to our bedroom to read. We couldn't sleep anyway, so we would spend four or five hours a night going through it all, crying, laughing, and crying again.

The letters were amazing, especially from kids Christina's age. Often they would include lines like, "She inspired me to play baseball, run for student council, volunteer at homeless shelters, give up my birthday money and tell people that instead of buying me a gift, give the money to the Christina-Taylor Green Foundation."

Kids who still had Christmas money left over sent it to the Foundation. I could feel the love in every note. It was as if this terrible tragedy was bringing people together. That didn't make it any easier, because so many of the gifts people made and sent incorporated Christina-Taylor's picture. And warm and cared for as that made me feel, it also reminded me that I had lost her and she wasn't coming back.

> **John:** *I continue to be amazed at what we get from people all over the country. We hear from other people who have lost children, from someone who appreciates our love for our country in spite of what we've been through, or someone who just wants to compliment us on how we've kept our composure.*
>
> *Because of Christina-Taylor's love for animals, we get hundreds of stuffed animals. We've got baseballs and bats with her name carved in them. And we hear from people who appreciate that she was an organ donor.*
>
> *Hard as it has been, it helps me to imagine Christina-Taylor looking down from heaven with a big smile because we have continued her dream of helping people. I never get tired of talking about my girl.*

But while the piercing sting of loss may have abated since those awful first weeks, the deep ache of mourning remains. I can't imagine it ever going away. Experts will say that the bereaved sometimes feel obligated to hang on to their grief, believing that to heal from it would somehow tarnish the memory of their loved one.

I don't feel obligated, and I don't believe John or Dallas do either. Because of who our loved one was, because of what she brought to our family, to our household, to our very lives, we have no choice. We cannot shake the sense of loss. I can now fully identify with parents I see on television true crime shows when they still tear up decades later at the way they lost their children.

It doesn't make sense to compare ways in which one could lose a child, but there is something unique about the senselessness of random murder. It's so sudden, so devastating that you feel as if you have been permanently knocked off balance. Regardless of what we do—and we give ourselves wholly to honoring Christina-Taylor's memory—we don't expect to ever regain the footing we had when our family was complete and our princess was in our home.

The summer of 2011 was particularly difficult because John's work took him to many of Christina-Taylor's favorite places. It was hard to be in Cape Cod and watch other kids build sand castles, play, swim, and go crabbing on the beach. My heart ached for Dallas, who now had to find other kids to play with because his sister was gone.

Visiting New York City didn't seem the same either, because Christina-Taylor loved it so. And to see *Mary Poppins* without her was almost unbearable. She would have enjoyed it so much. It was painful not to see her in our hotel room.

There is a certain, almost scary, quiet in our home now. When we returned from our trip east, I noticed we hadn't taken as many pictures as we used to. Things are just not the same without our lovely daughter.

I still find it hard to go into her room, so I just don't. It's too hard. At some point early on, Heidi Garrett helped me clean it out, and that was torture. I kept a few special things and gave her good clothes and shoes to her godmother's daughter, Hailey Grant. Most of the rest went to the Salvation Army or Goodwill.

John: To this day I often wake up in the morning and expect Christina-Taylor to be there. I expect her to go hang out with me, ask me what are we doing today, hiking, swimming, what? It's a fresh grief every day.

The sting maybe isn't as sharp as it once was, but it's always there. There are constant reminders. Going to a hotel we all enjoyed. Leafing through photo albums. She always took such a beautiful picture.

Boy, I miss her big brown eyes and that smile when I would come home from the road, having been gone three weeks and dog tired. Then I would hear her: "Daddy's home!" She'd come out grinning and run to me for her hug and kiss, and all that tiredness would just go away. Knowing I'll never have that again is a tough thing to overcome. She could fire me up with her enthusiasm for me just getting home.

We've talked about how fortunate we were that Dallas had karate that day or we might have lost him too. The thing is, if they both went, Roxanna might have gone too. I could have lost my whole family. I don't even like to think about that. I can't imagine anything being worse than losing one.

For Roxanna and me, we just have to be there for each other. You never know what's going to trigger a low in either one of us. Maybe it'll be looking at old photos or just the quiet of the house without the two kids playing or carousing or fighting. Maybe the empty spot at the table.

Then we just talk about how much we miss her, and when Roxanna is really down, I just hold her and comfort her by reminding her that Christina-Taylor will be remembered for making her mark on the world, and that she is in heaven and happy there.

We still have not let anger creep in, but a heavy sadness is always just below the surface. Our faith has played such an important role in helping us through. We pray. We get together with family and friends. And we hang on.

I ask God for the strength to carry on, to relieve the burden of grief on Roxanna and Dallas, and to take good care of Christina. I know He does. Nothing can harm her in heaven. But it feels good to ask anyway.

A lot of times family and friends don't know that I'm hurting, and that's okay. I'm not trying to hide anything, but I don't want to burden them. And just being close to them is comforting.

I also find it comforting to speak to Christina. I just tell her we have work yet to do down here but that I am eager to see her and join her one day in heaven. That's very emotional but also healing.

I love thinking about Christina-Taylor and will do so forever.

<hr />

As for me, sometimes it feels as if I am hanging by my fingertips at the edge of a cliff. There are good days and bad days.

At the beginning, of course, it was horrible, horrendous. I couldn't even believe it was happening. And then with the added pressure of the tragedy being so public, well if anything it made it worse. If her death hadn't been part of a mass murder at a political meeting, if she hadn't been the youngest victim, if her grandfather was not Dallas Green, if, if, if . . .

I can't say how much easier it might have been if this had not been a national event, but as honored as we were to see her gain the attention of the country and even the president, we were in no condition to appreciate that. Everybody was calling and coming and helping and consoling, and we had hardly been able to process the reality of it yet. You go from a happy little idyllic family one day to being the center of attention the next—and for all the wrong reasons.

I felt for the first little while that I was consoling others as much as they were consoling me. It wasn't the normal grief process, of that I'm sure.

Now, like John, I just have that daily nagging feeling that something, someone, is missing. She was social and happy and she and Dallas played noisily together. I don't hear her singing. I can't dance with her. She gave me a kiss and a hug every day when she came home from school.

It's the quiet I have to learn to live with, to get used to.

For a long time, I felt as if I were functioning at half speed. I did all the things I had to do, but I wasn't at my best. I didn't worry about it. I was like, *Who cares? There's a little more dust—little things that aren't getting done the way they should—but we're going through a horrible time.*

I'm finally getting my rest, but I have suffered a wound that time will not heal. I look at pictures of her and it's painful. It's just sad. I see children her age finishing one school year and looking forward to the next. I dream of what might have been for a girl so enthusiastic about life, so energetic, so passionate about everything. She had such a promising future, was bright, and a hard worker. We got robbed. She got robbed.

Every day I think about her. And I'm not angry as much as sad, sad she didn't get to fulfill her dreams. I feel sad when I see girls who look like Christina-Taylor. They remind me of the terrible loss and how a beautiful and near-perfect life was snuffed out. We had so many plans and will never be able to do all the amazing things we discussed.

She was beyond her years and had already planned her Sweet Sixteen party (nearly half her life away), her graduation party, and even her college choice.

But when I'm at my lowest, I remember what her loving father said at her funeral, that Christina-Taylor would want everybody to know that everything was going to be okay. That was her. The ringleader. The peacemaker. The best way I can honor her legacy is to remember what kind of character she had. If something bad happened, she would endure her moment of sadness and then regroup. She was a gamer. That's how she was.

Yeah, sometimes I'm still a basket case, and I'm going to cry every night. But Christina-Taylor was strong—strong willed and always seeing the positive in things. She wouldn't let us be down. She would want us to move on and do positive things in her memory. And she really wouldn't want us to dwell on the ugliness, the sad part.

And so I pray and think of my beautiful Christina-Taylor every day. I pray for extra strength on days when I feel the worst. I ask God to help me get through the day and for the strength to be the kind of parent and wife Dallas and John deserve. I thank God for all the wonderful things He has given us and for the strength to make good things happen through our foundation.

I know God needed my daughter to do great things in heaven, and I try to think of what she must be doing and the fun times she must be having with Grandma. When God sent her to me in my dream, she told me she was happy, so I hang on to that thought with everything that's in me.

John: The tragedy that sent Christina-Taylor to heaven stirred the nation to its very foundation. And after witnessing the outpouring of love and genuine desire for change from around this great land, I truly believe our country can become as good as she imagined it.

Our little girl seemed to embody all that is good about America. We all need to believe that the American dream is still achievable and that by doing the simple things in life and doing them well, we all have the same opportunity to enjoy it.

We have learned through this ordeal that by getting back to our roots, we can overcome anything and that there are many good people among us. What a shame that it took a tragedy for us to find that out.

Being involved with our family, with our church, with our friends, and our community—that is the gift and lasting legacy Christina-Taylor has left us. She has shown others that their hopes and dreams can come alive if they take the steps to live them out. And she has shown that by caring for others who are less fortunate, we can make the world a better place.

We miss her dearly, but we know she will not be forgotten.

We are proud that our angel left a profound mark on this world for others to follow. I hope that by our telling this story, others will understand not only the grief and sorrow we experienced, but also feel our love for her and pride in her as we witness the impact of her character and deeds. That is how her legacy will live on.

I want people to never forget Christina-Taylor and the way she lived her life—that she was born on 9/11/01 and died on that tragic day, 1/8/11. While those were both dark days, the nine years of her life in between were beautiful, and she knew and said often how lucky we were as a family.

Many parents have told me that hearing her story has made them hold their kids a little tighter, to treasure each day and cherish the time they have with their loved ones.

It is Christina-Taylor's hope, her ambition, her dreams, her spirit of life that keep us going and will be her legacy. I think she would want people to remember her as a fierce competitor and a strong little woman. She was brave and adventurous, she wanted to learn, she wanted to help people, and she wanted to make a difference.

I hope by my telling her story, she has accomplished just that.

NOTES

Chapter 13: The Outpouring

1. White House press office transcript; accessed online at http://www.whitehouse.gov/the-press-office/2011/01/12/ remarks-president-barack-obama-memorial-service-victims -shooting-tucson

Chapter 14: In Remembrance

1. Composed by Franz Schubert, 1826; lyricist unknown.

2. Lyrics by John Newton, 1779.

3. Lyrics are the property of Billy Joel, from the album *River of Dreams*, 1993. Used by permission.

4. Personal correspondence from Billy Joel. Used by permission.

Chapter 16: Seeking Peace

1. White House press office transcript; accessed online at http://www.whitehouse.gov/the-press-office/2011/01/25/ remarks-president-state-union-address

Chapter 17: The Visitation

1. Personal correspondence from Peyton Manning. Used with permission.

ROXANNA GREEN has been a practicing home healthcare nurse who now serves as CEO of the Christina-Taylor Green Foundation (christina-taylorgreen.org). Her husband, John, is National Cross-checker in the scouting department of the Los Angeles Dodgers. They have a son, Dallas, 12, and their daughter, Christina-Taylor, would have been 10 on the tenth anniversary of 9/11.

JERRY B. JENKINS is a *New York Times* best-selling novelist (the Left Behind series) and biographer (Billy Graham, Hank Aaron, Walter Payton, Orel Hershiser, Nolan Ryan, Joe Gibbs, and many more), with over 70 million books sold. His writing has appeared in *Time*, *Reader's Digest*, *Parade*, *Guideposts*, and he has been featured on the cover of *Newsweek*.

WORTHY
PUBLISHING

IF YOU LIKED THIS BOOK . . .

- Tell your friends by going to: http://as-good-as-she-imagined.com and clicking "LIKE"

- Share the video book trailer by posting it on your Facebook page

- Head over to our Facebook page, click "LIKE" and post a comment regarding what you enjoyed about the book

- Tweet "I recommend reading #AsGoodAsSheImagined by @JerryBJenkins @Worthypub"

- Hashtag: #AsGoodAsSheImagined

- Subscribe to our newsletter by going to http://worthy-publishing.com/about/subscribe.php

**WORTHY PUBLISHING
FACEBOOK PAGE**

**WORTHY PUBLISHING
WEBSITE**